DADDY'S GIRL
COLORING BOOK

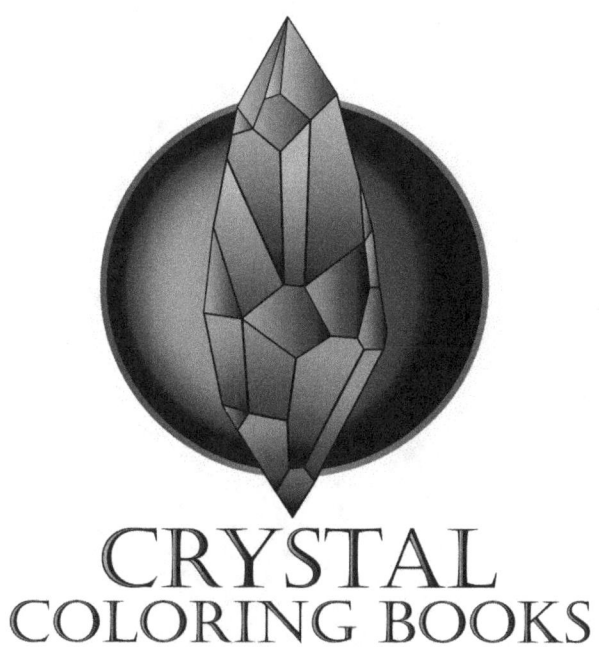

CRYSTAL
COLORING BOOKS

ISBN-13:: 978-1722777043
ISBN-10: 1722777044

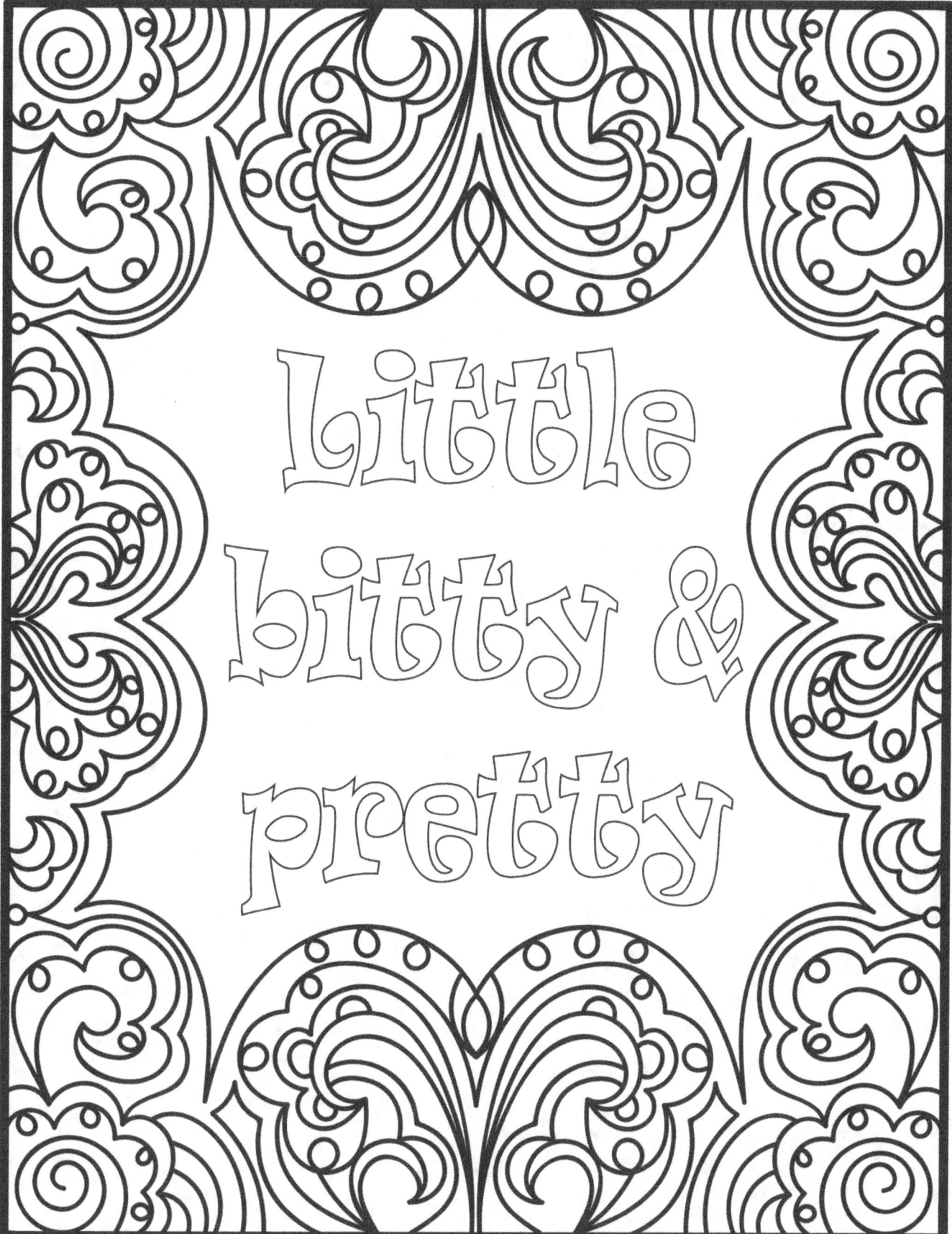

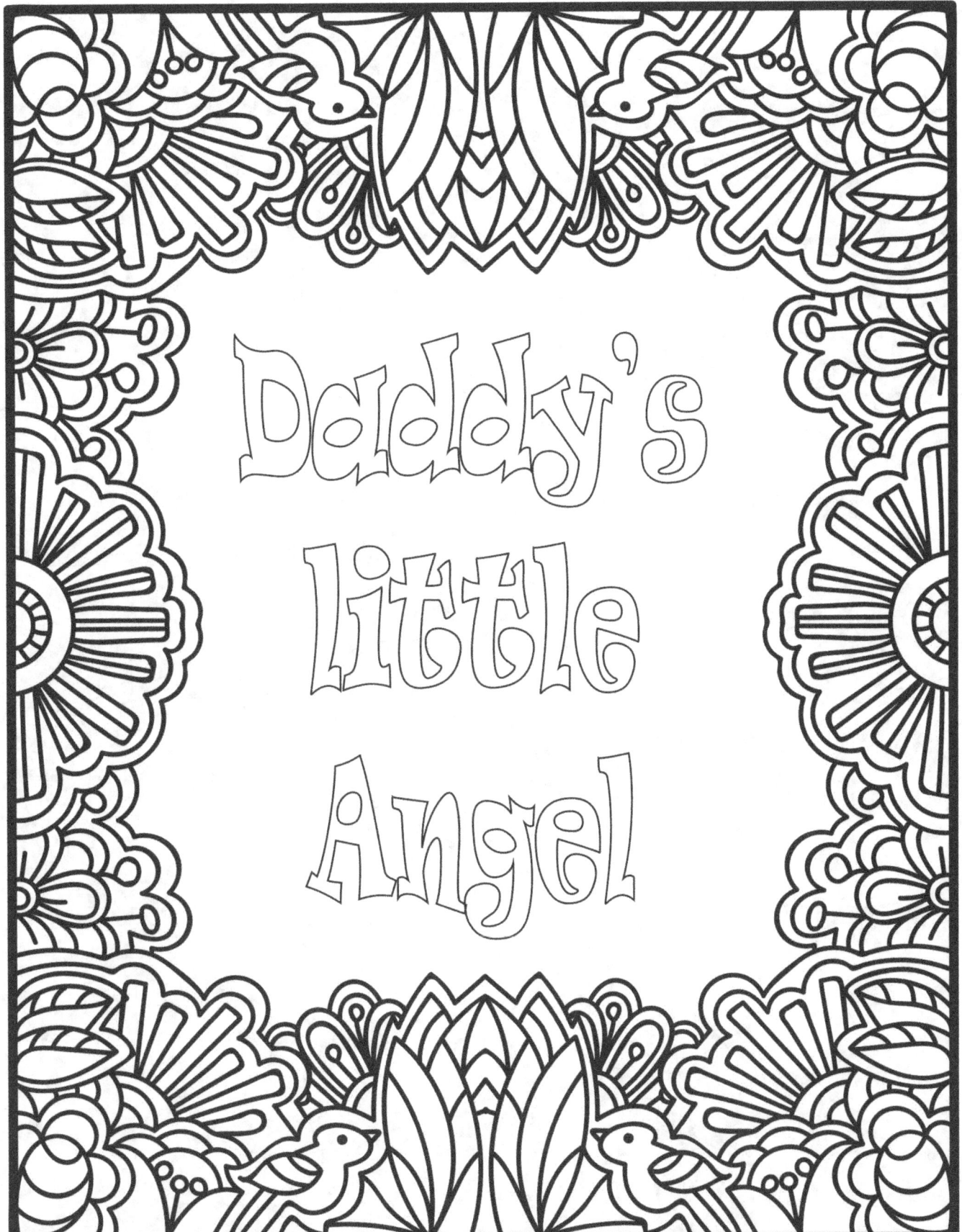

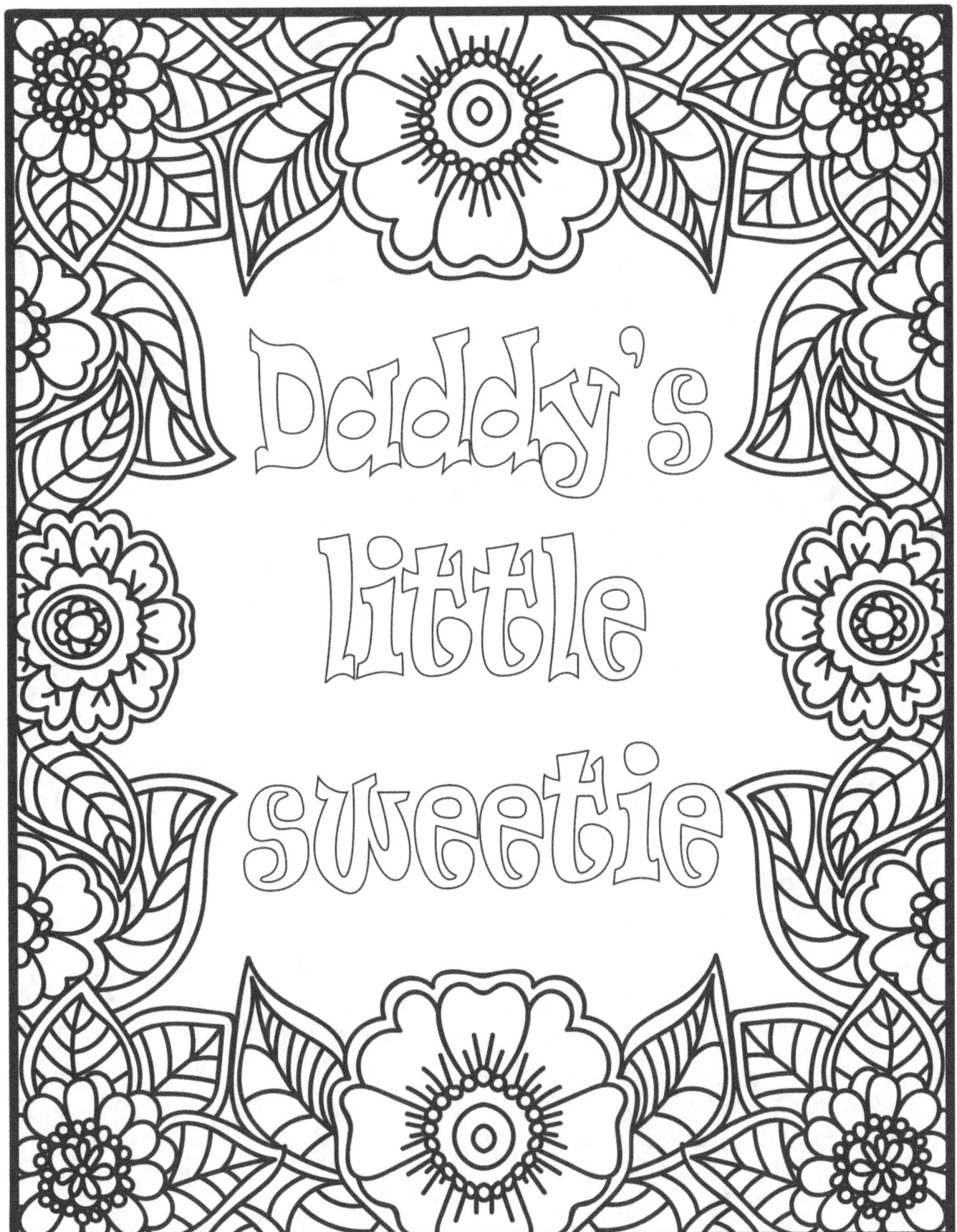

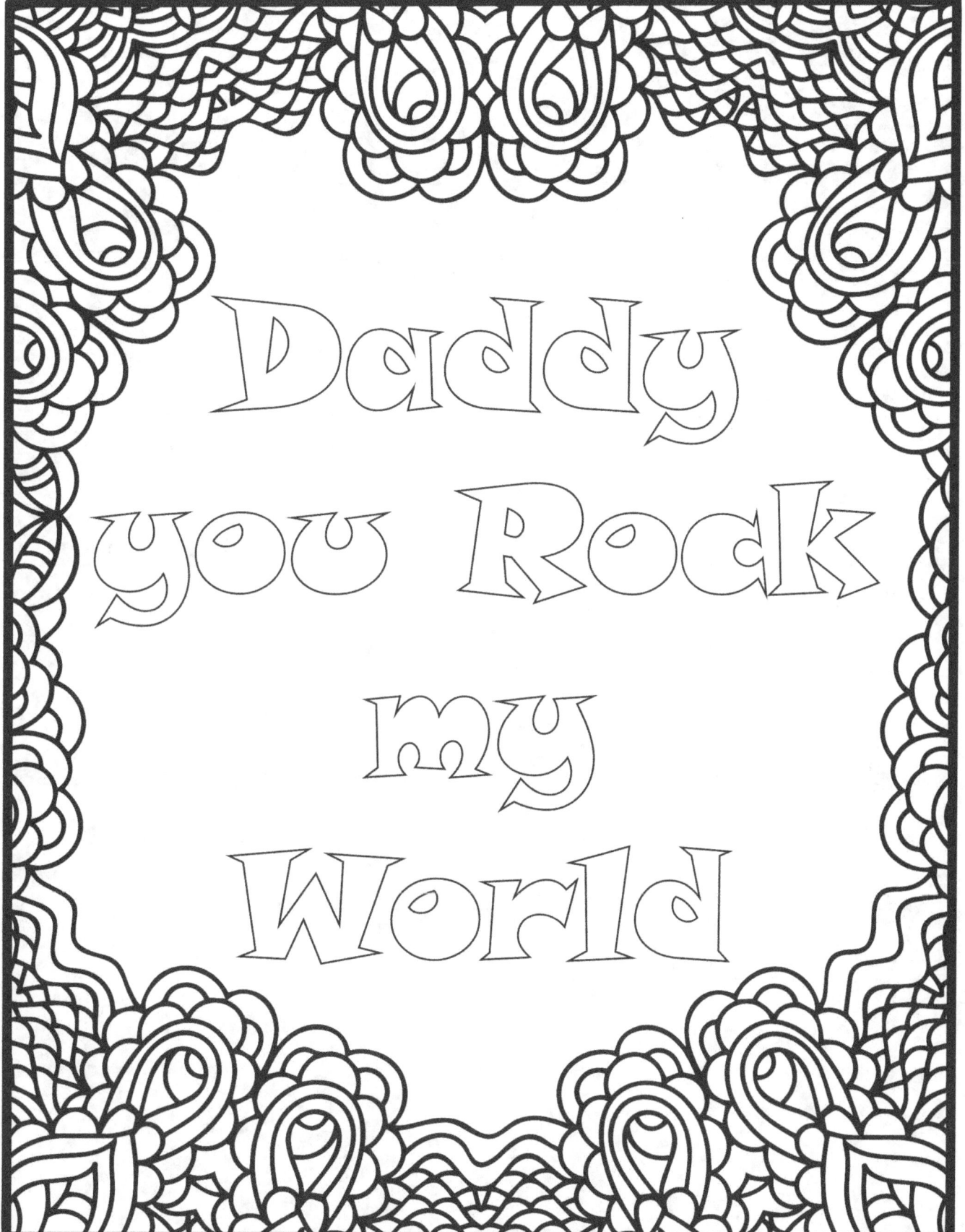

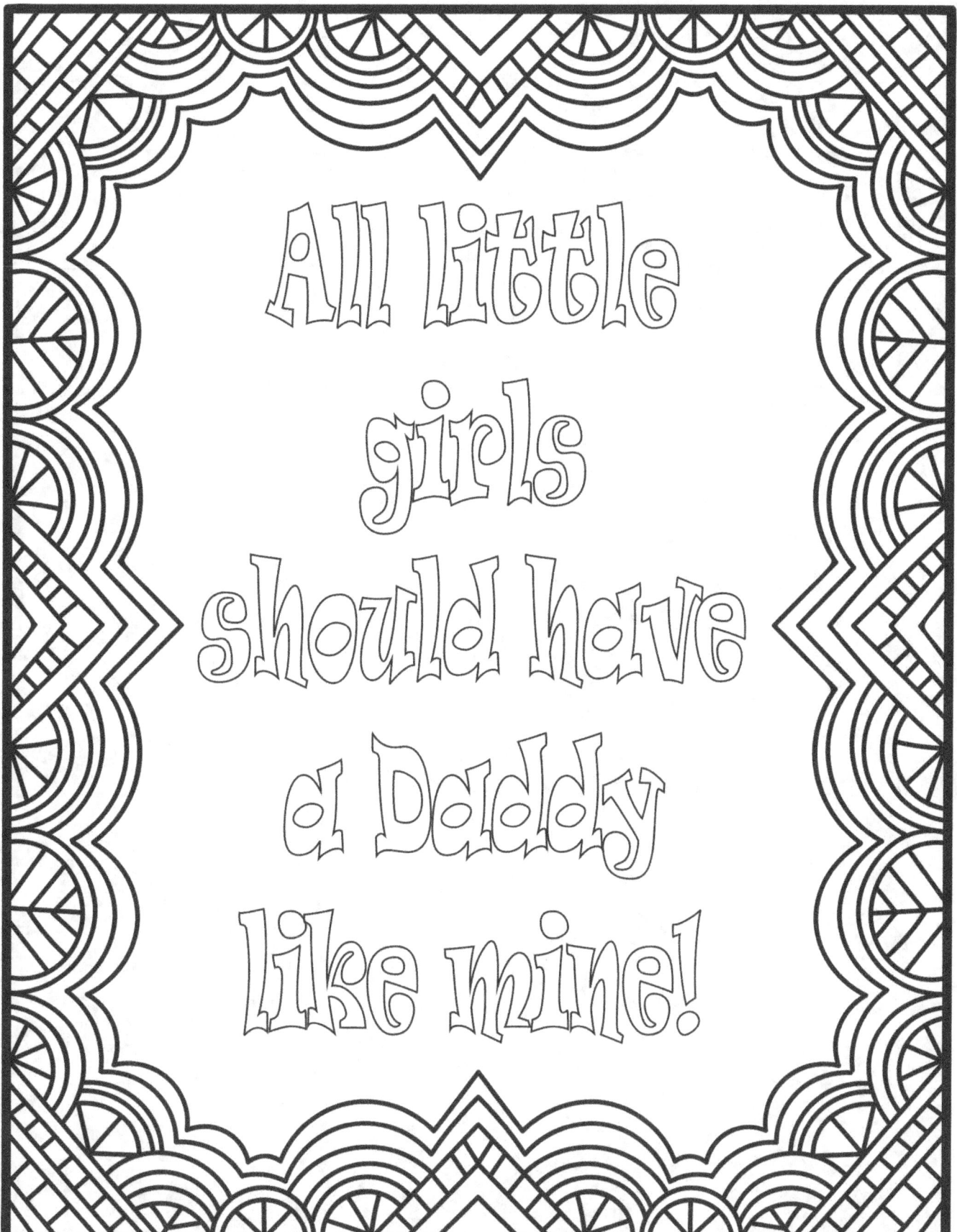

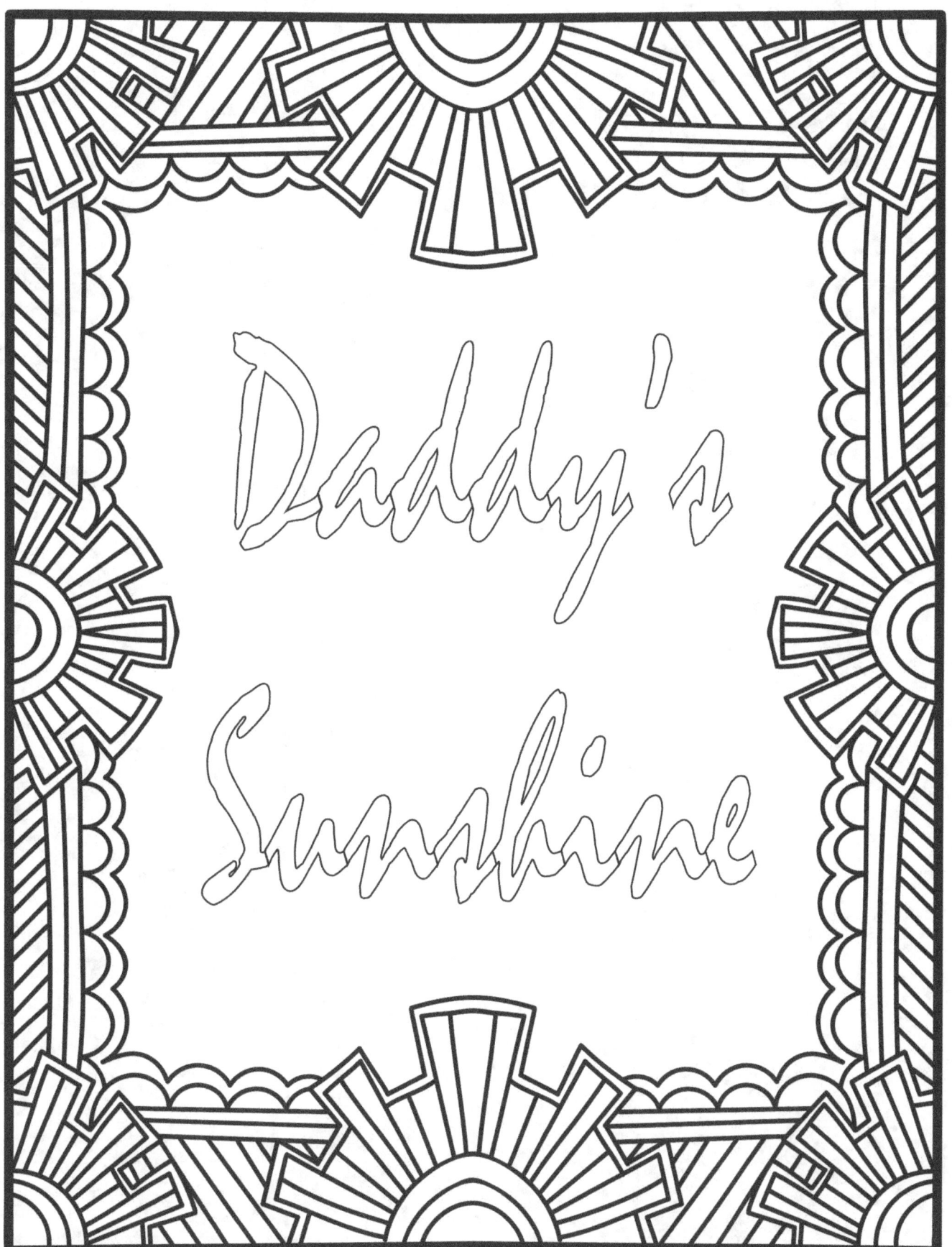

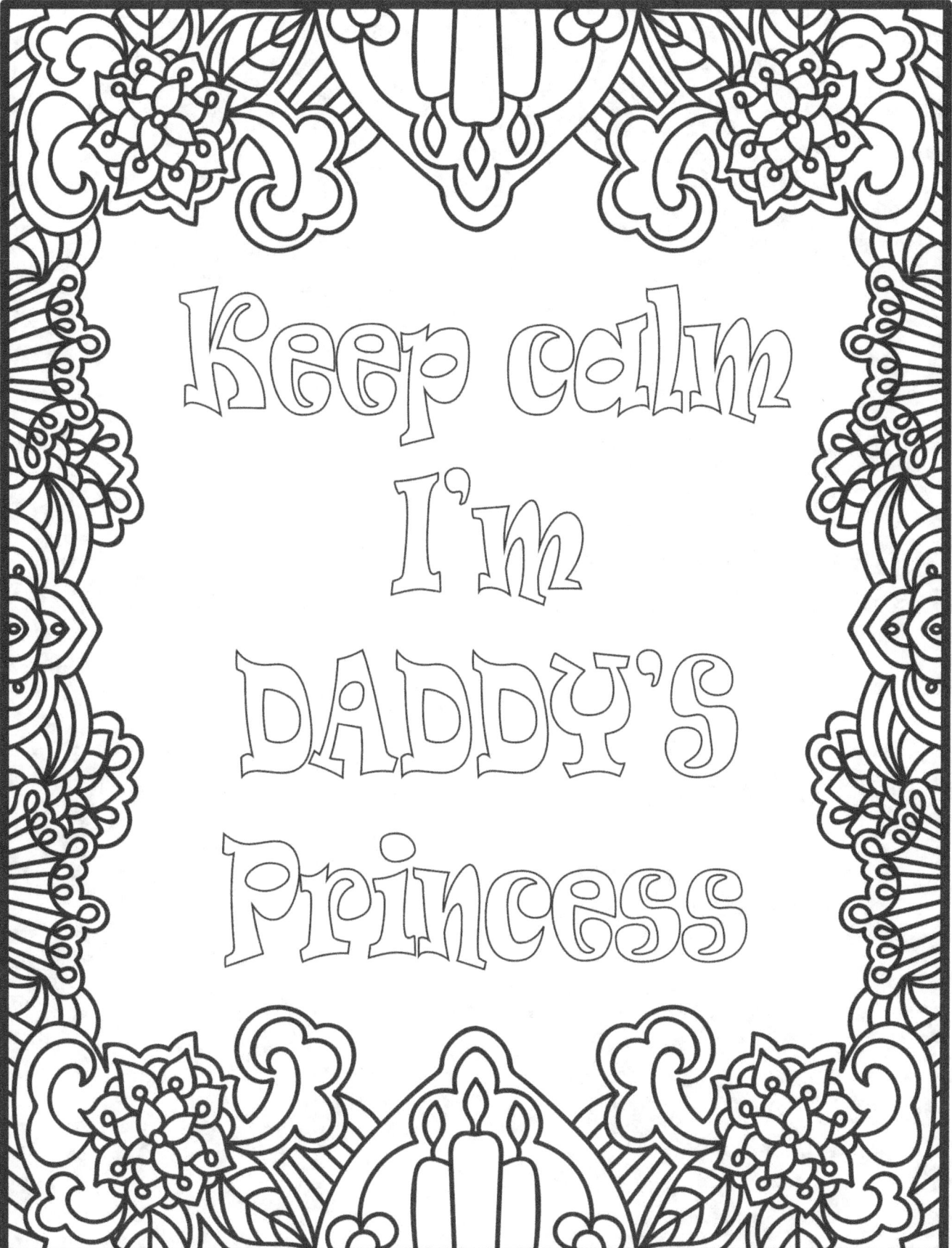

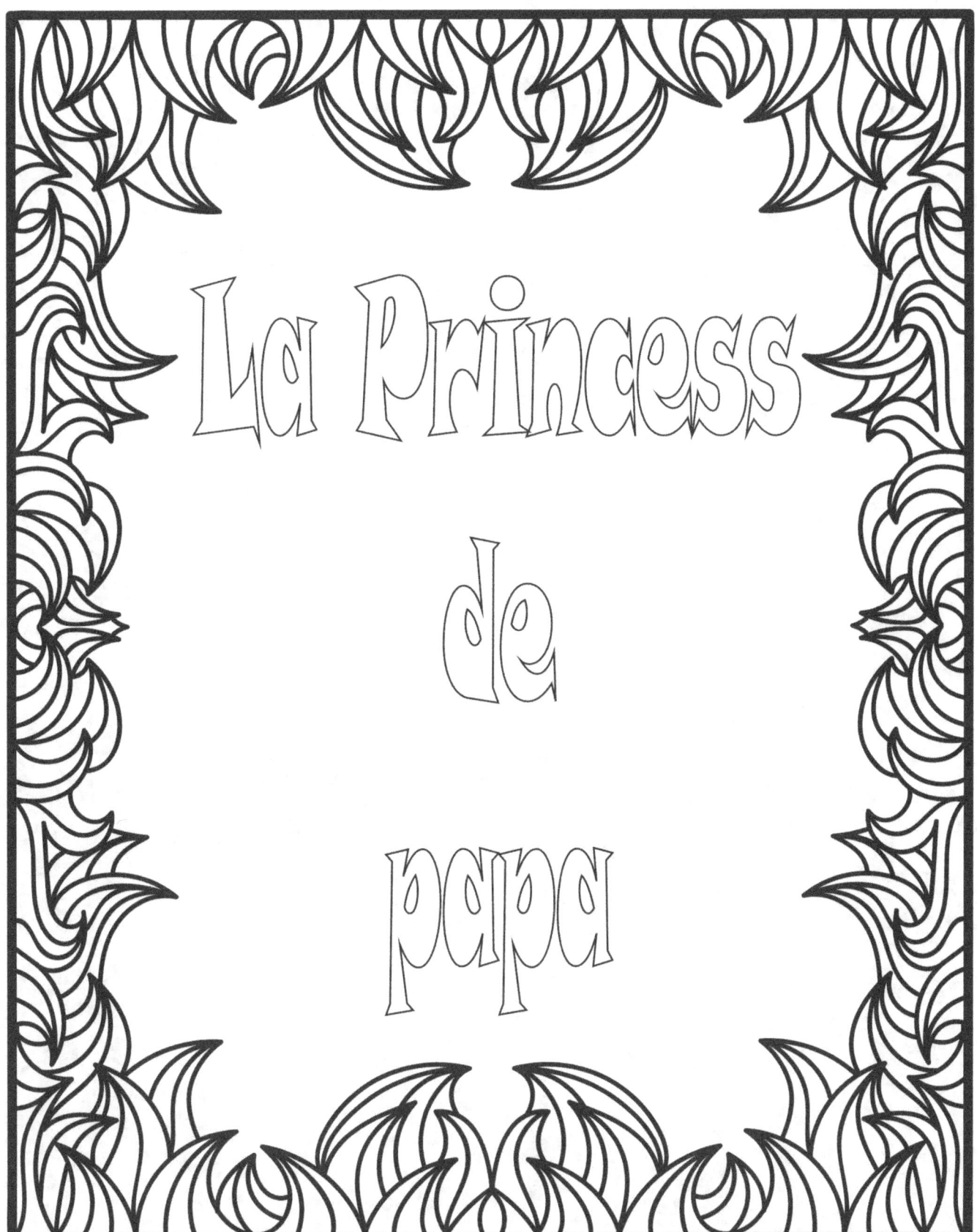

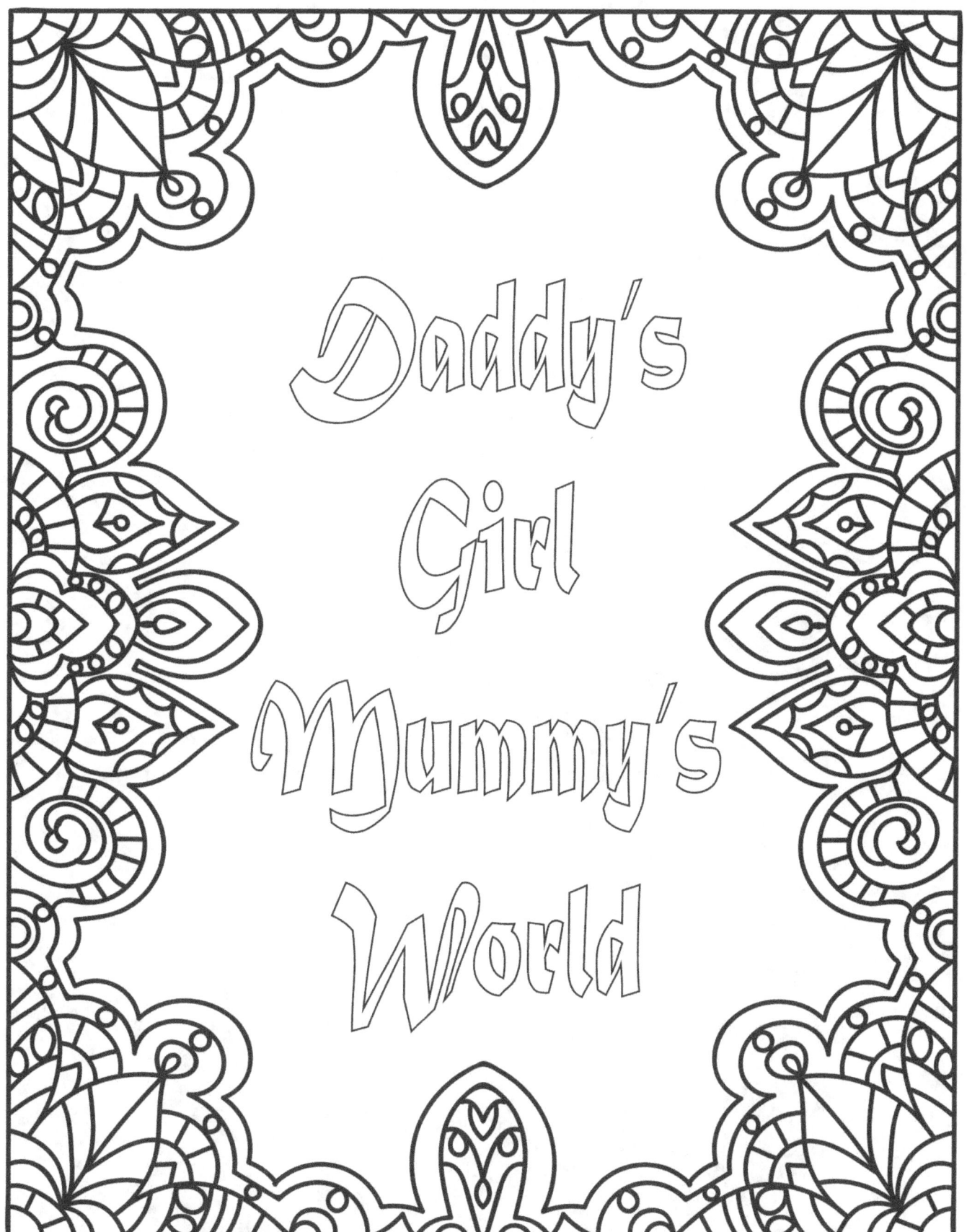

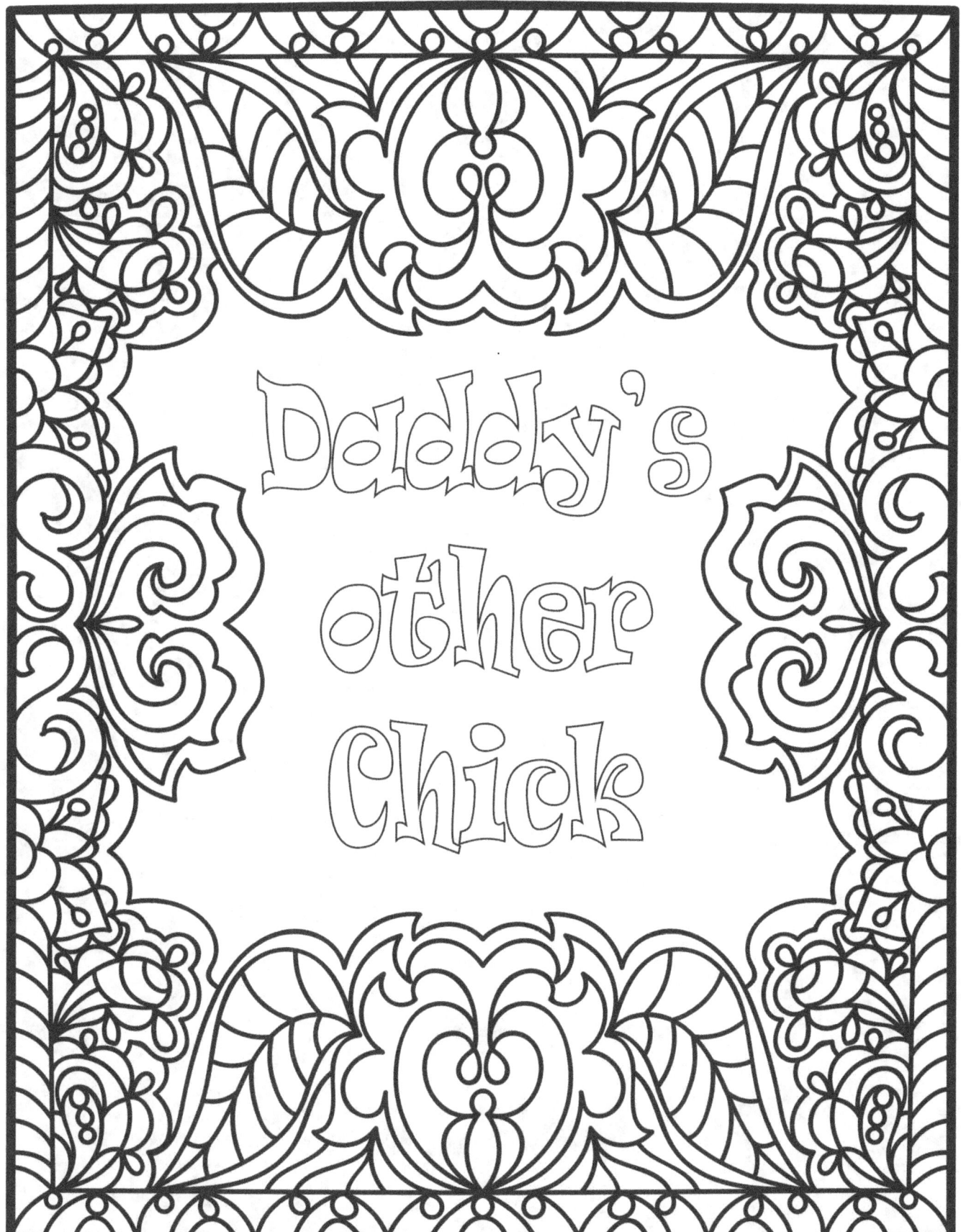

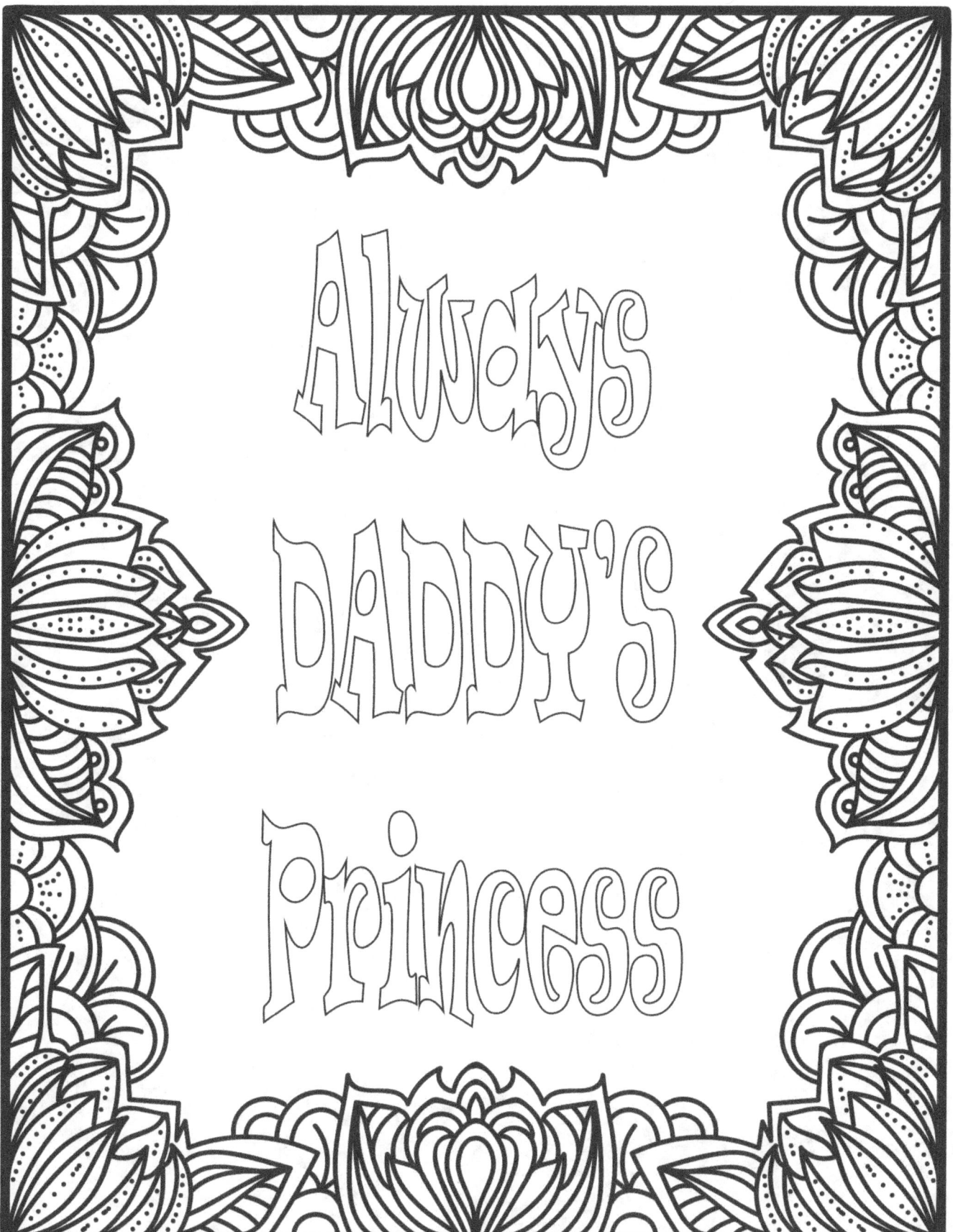

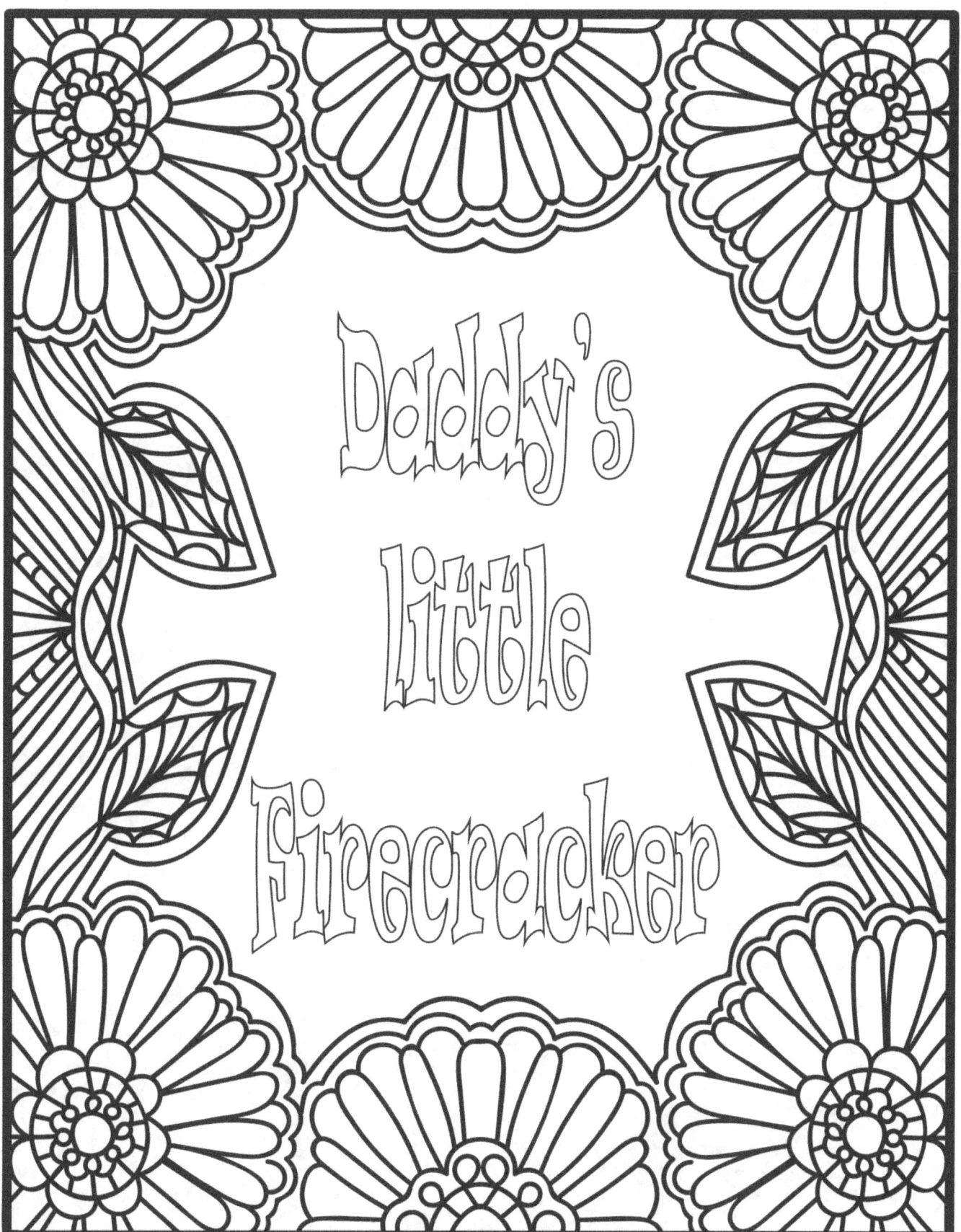

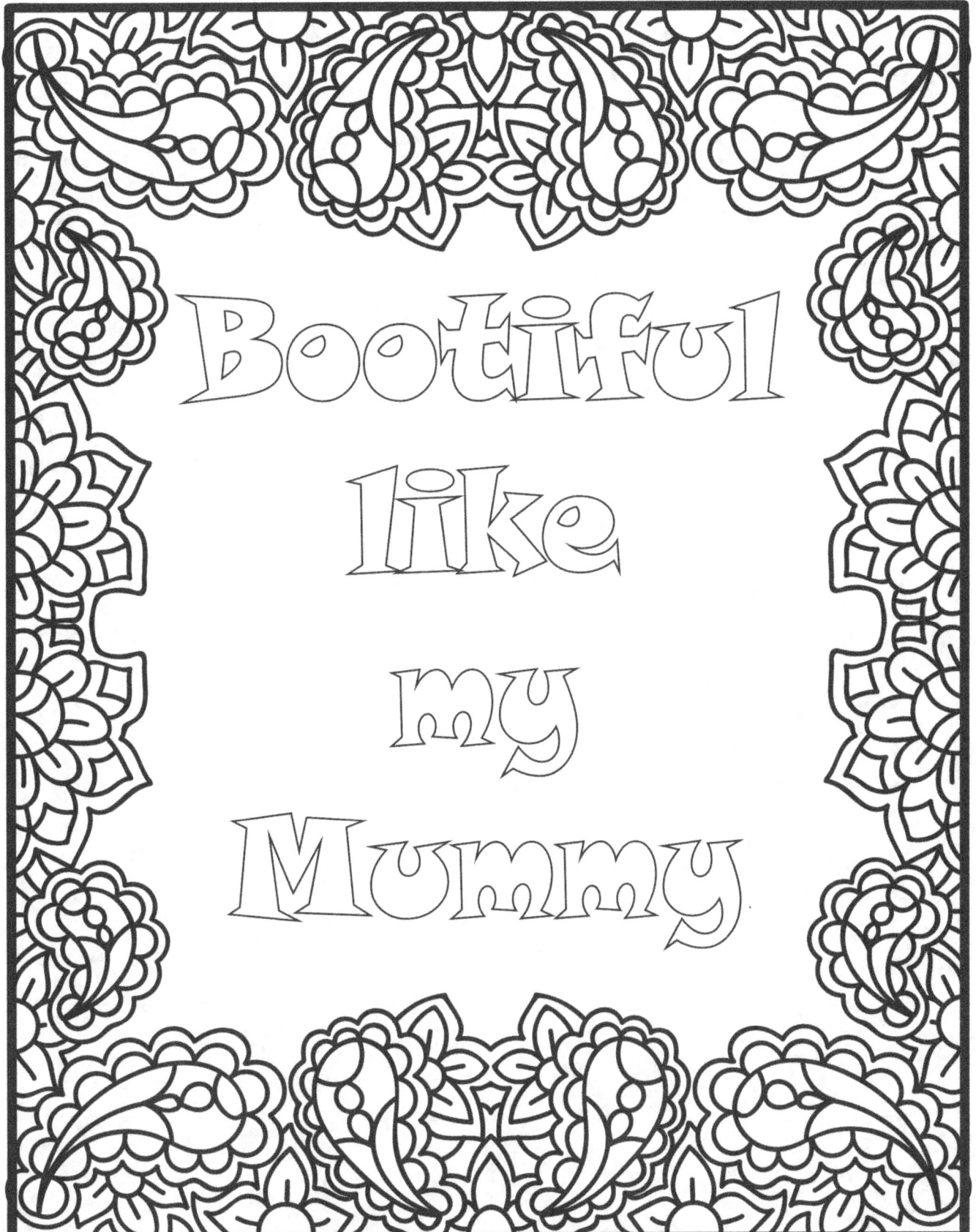

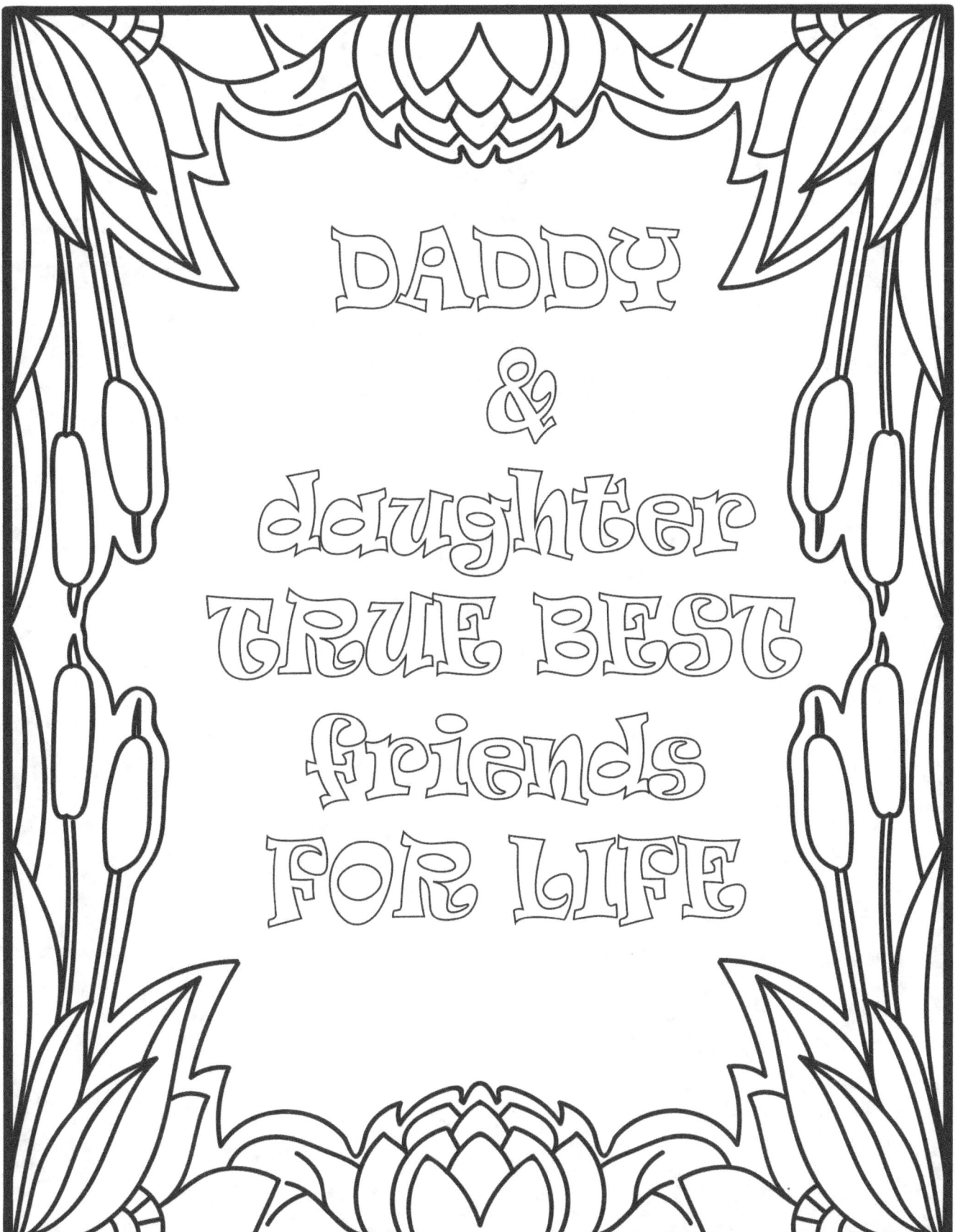

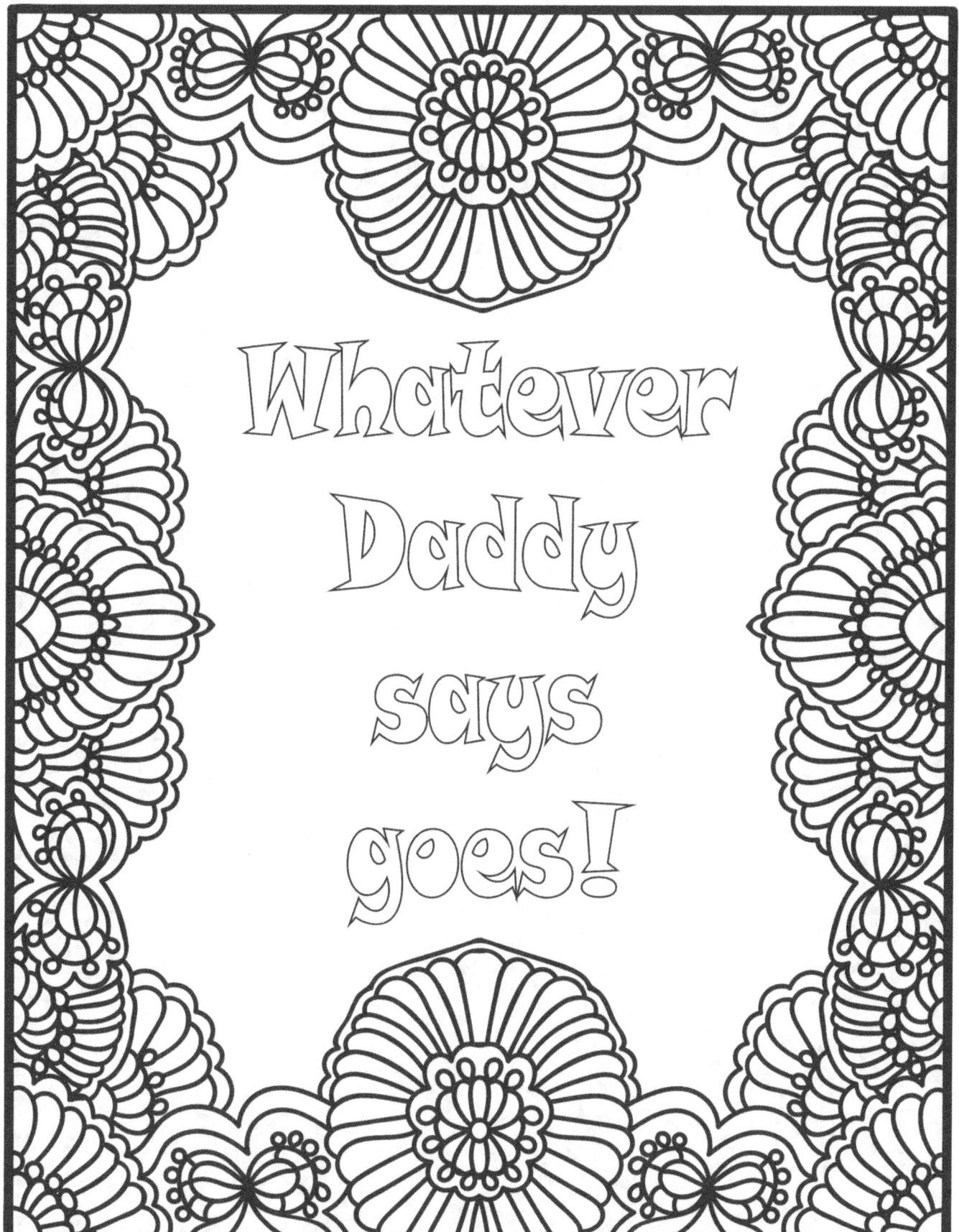

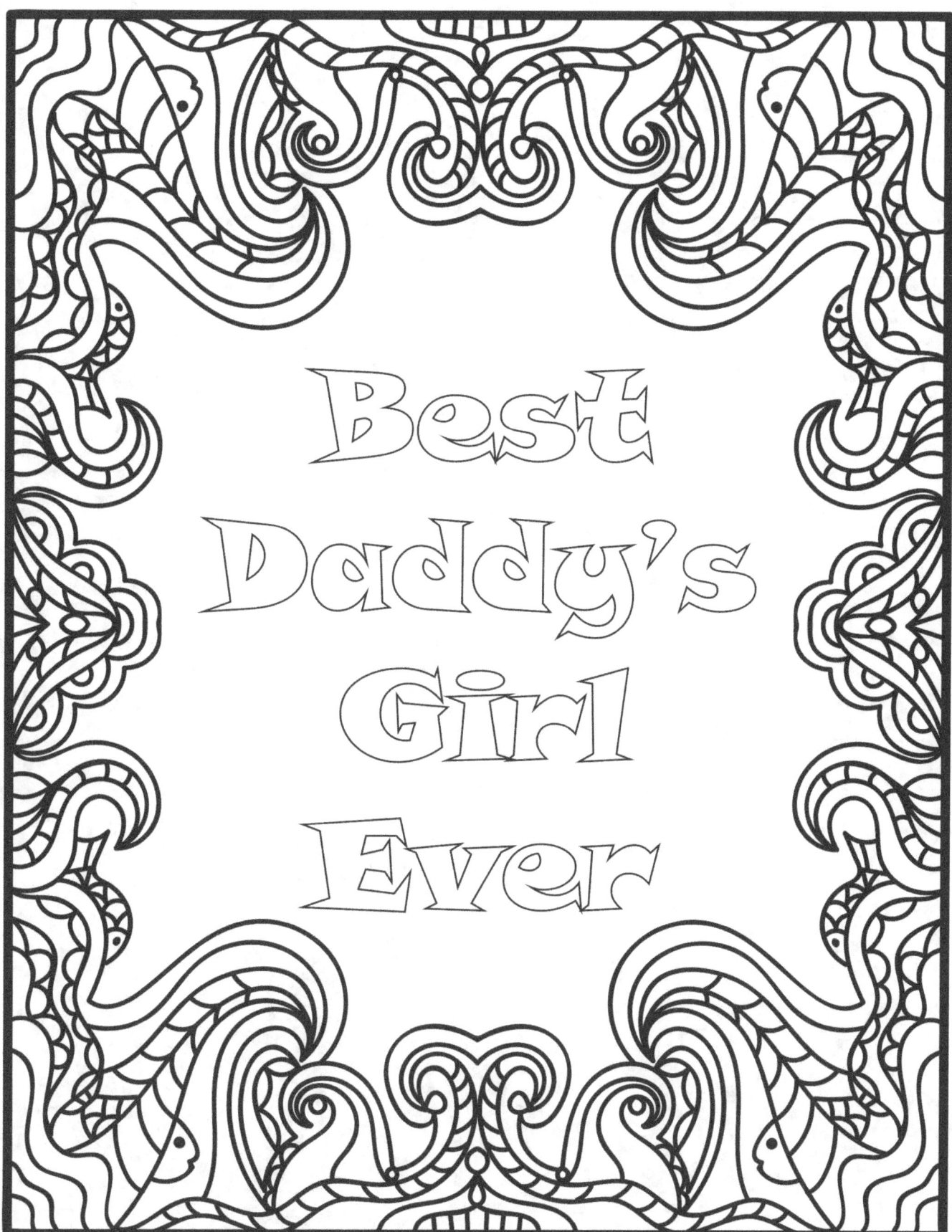

I found
my
Prince
his name
is
DADDY

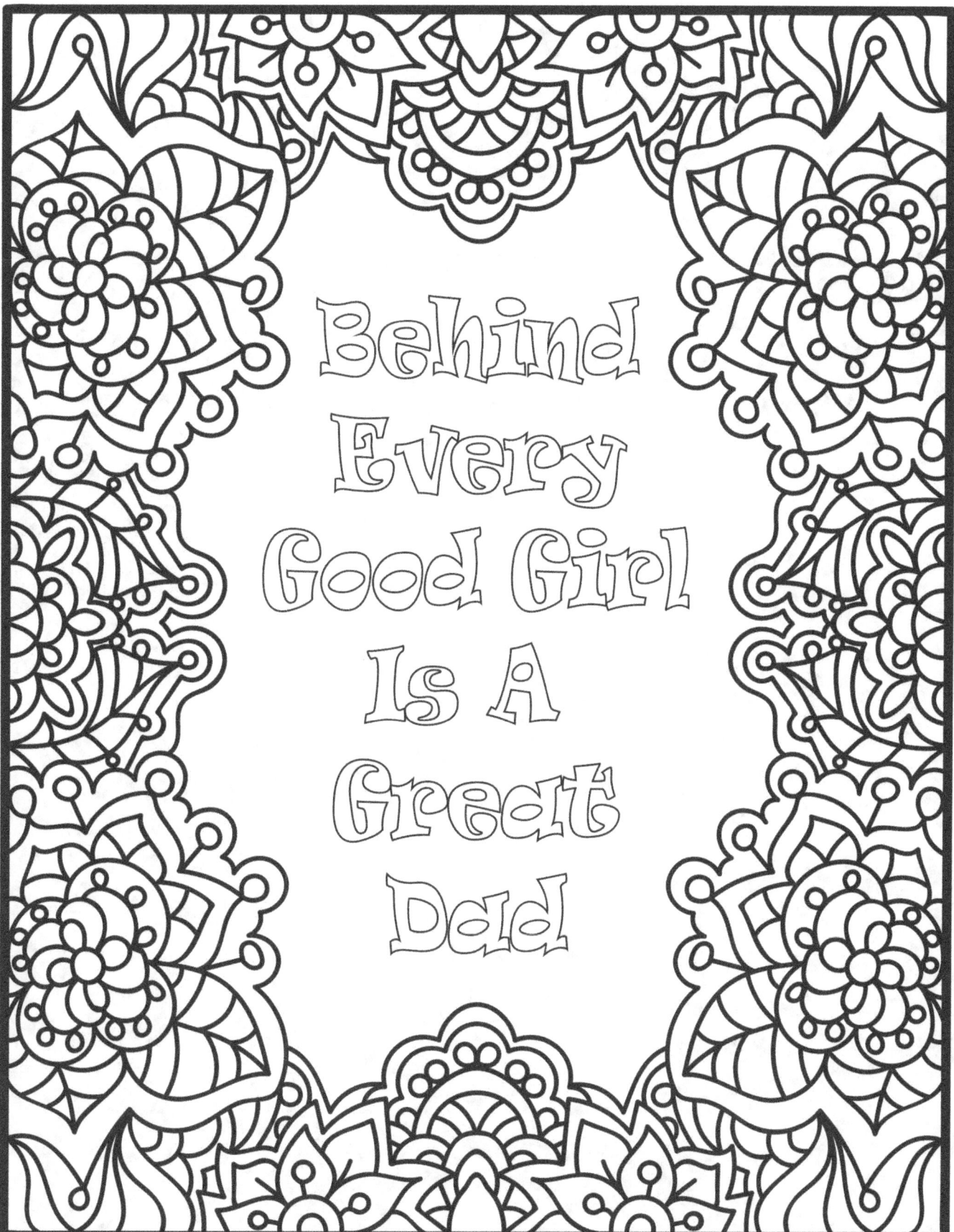

Behind Every Good Girl Is A Great Dad

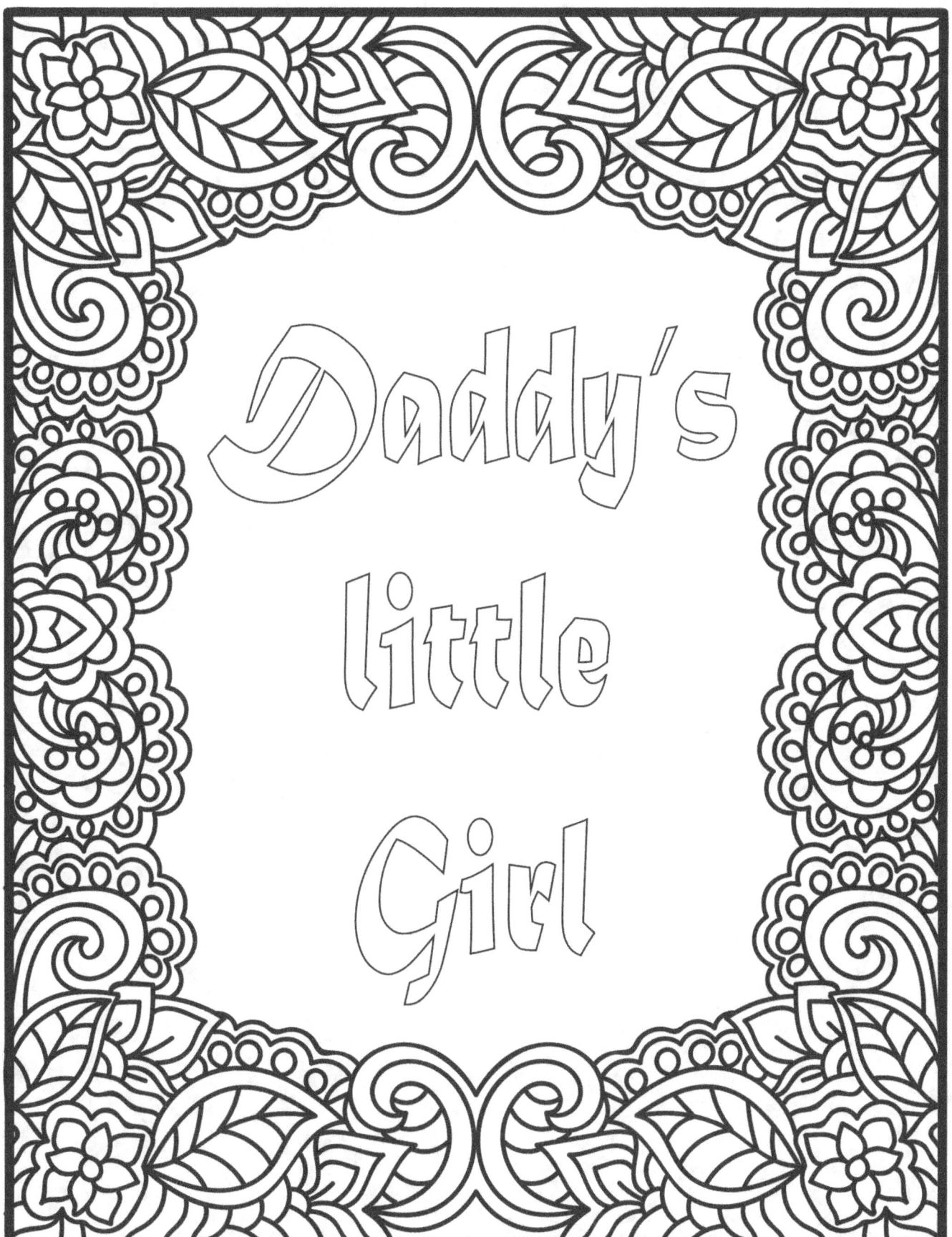

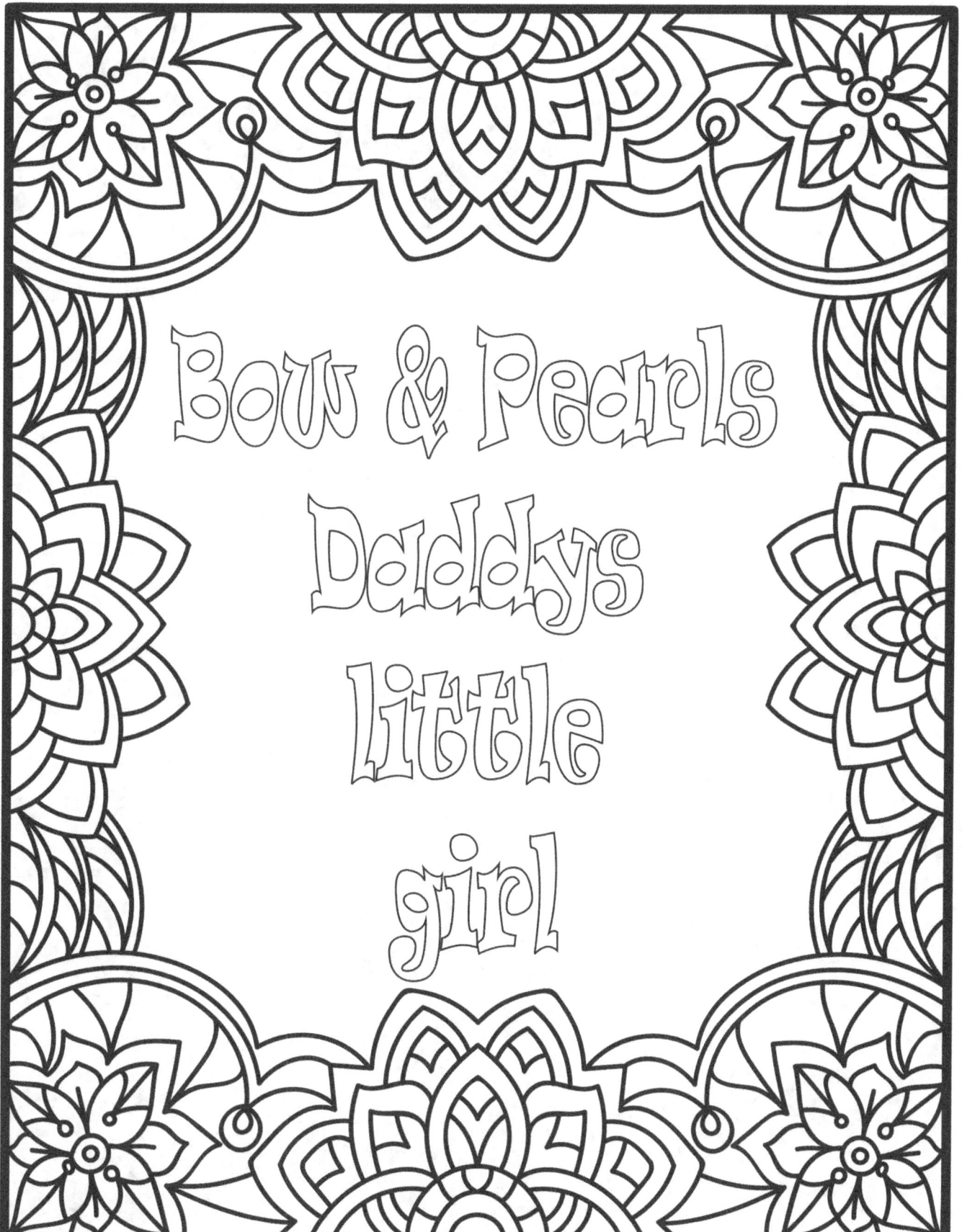

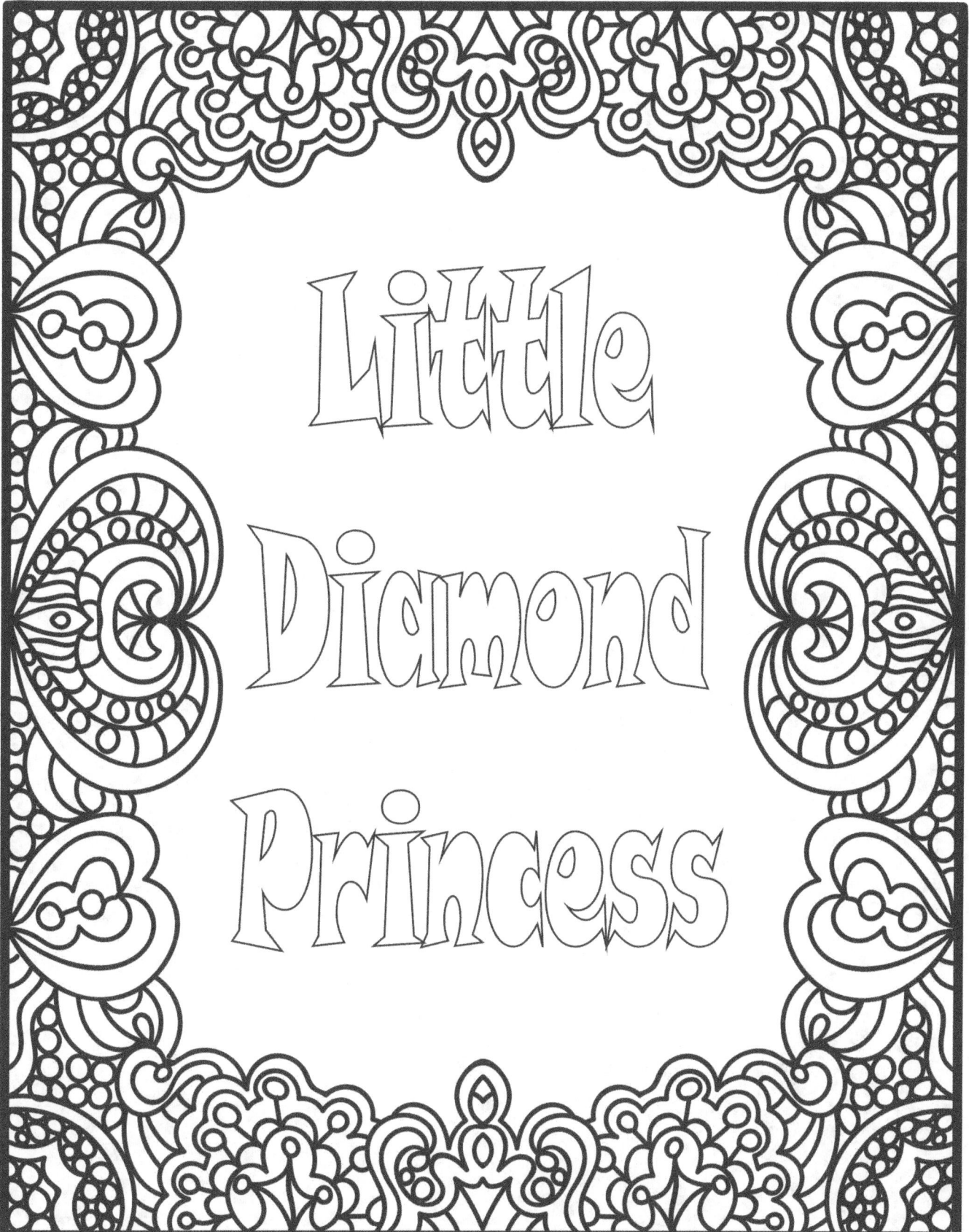

My Daddy's Perfect Princess

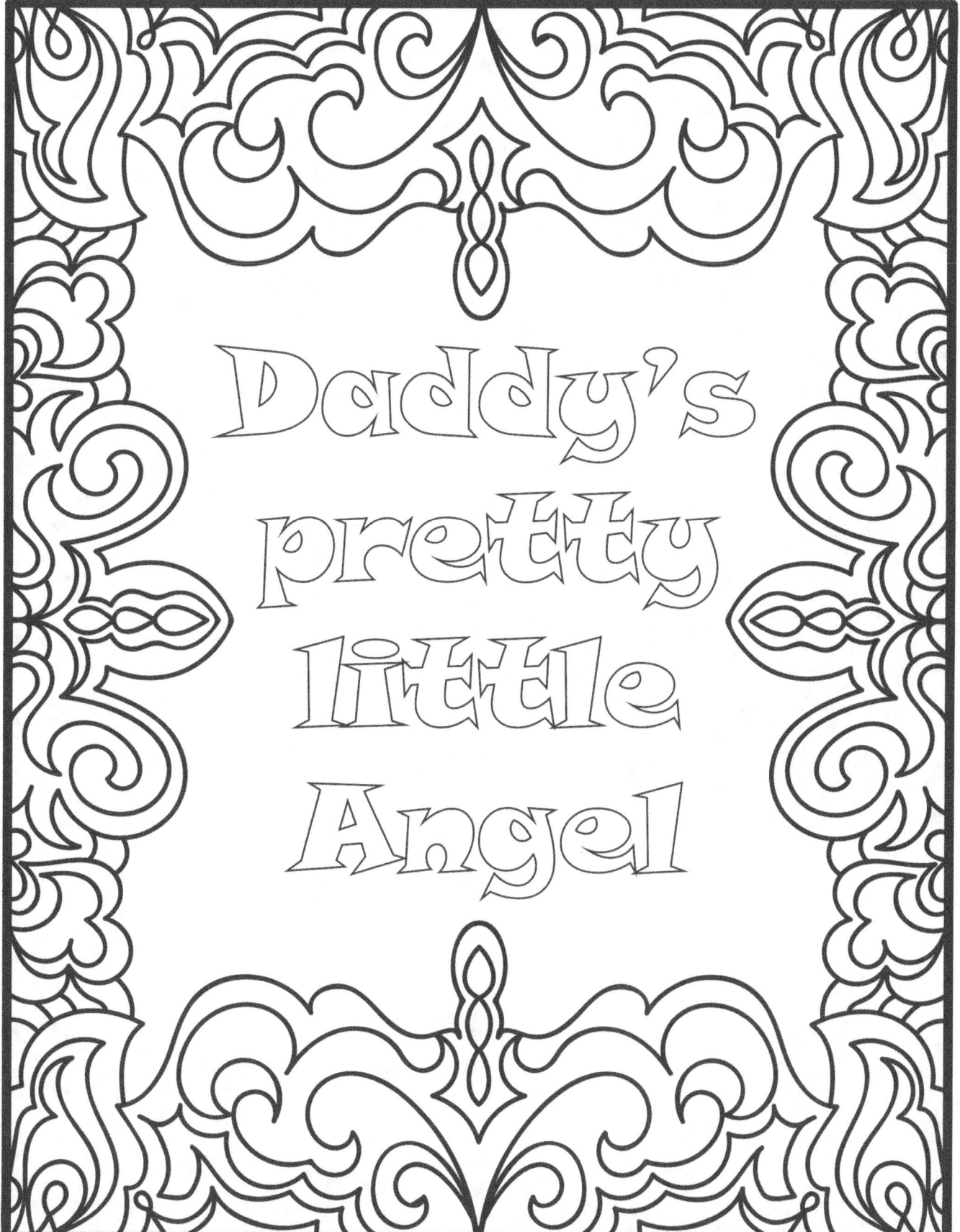

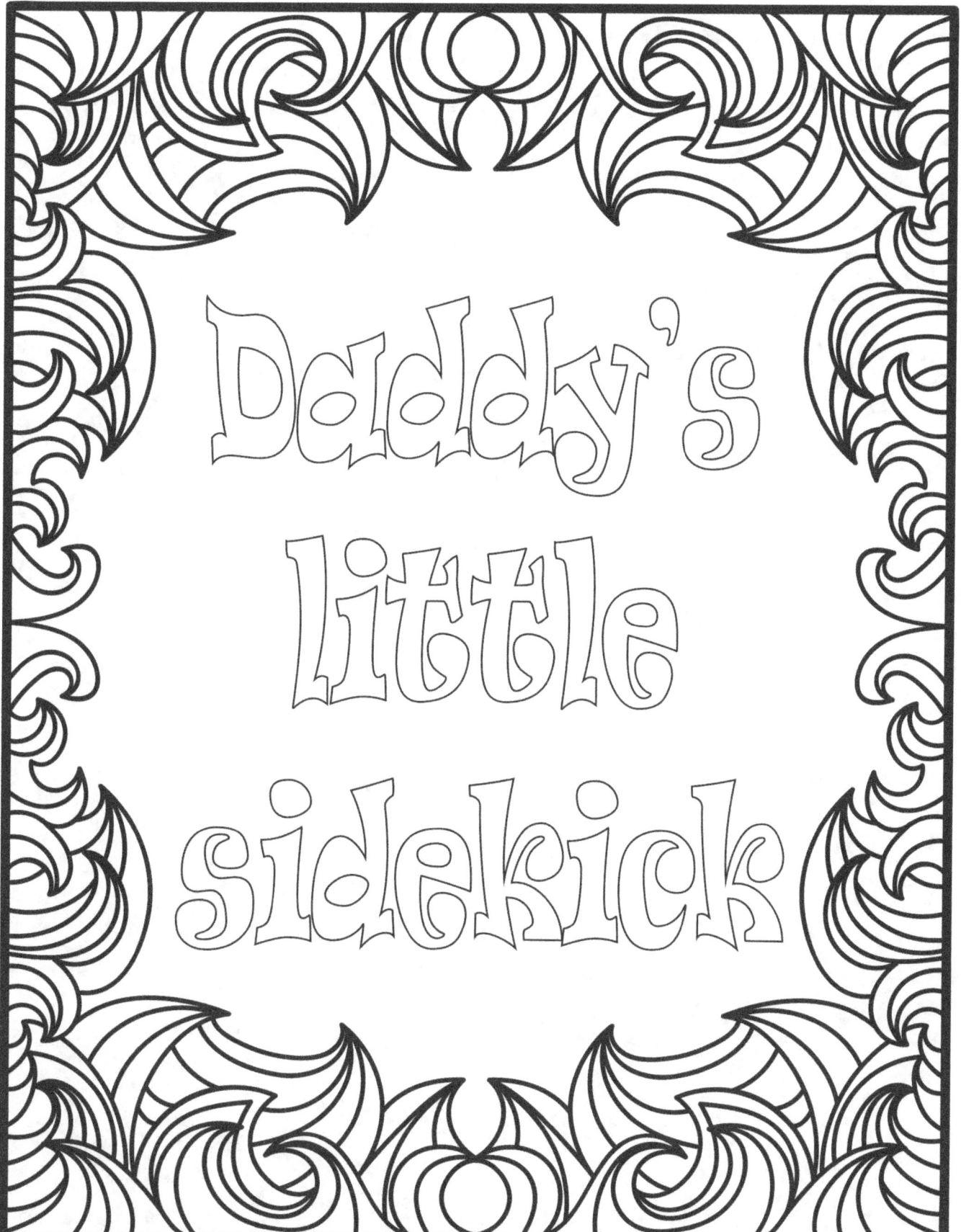

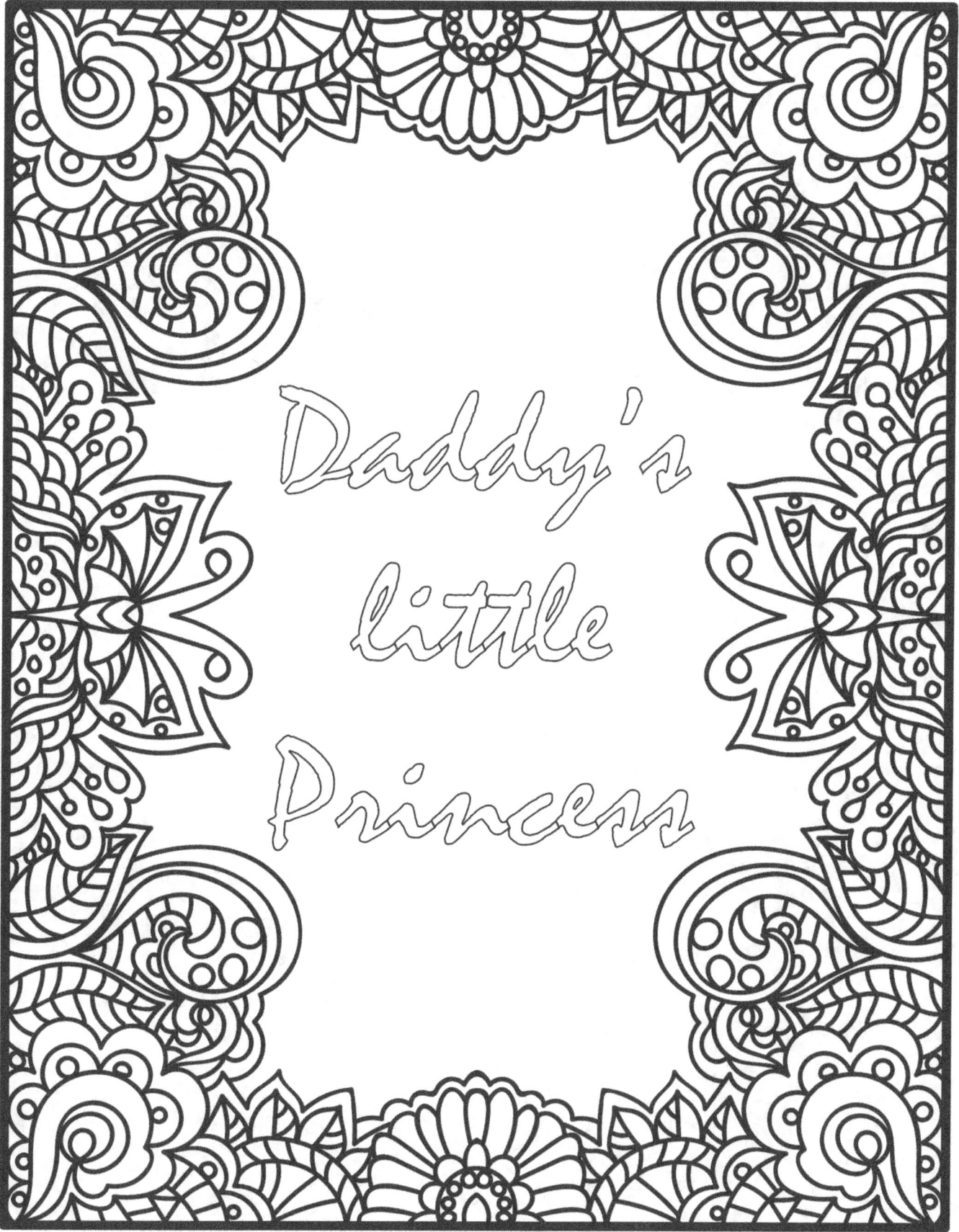

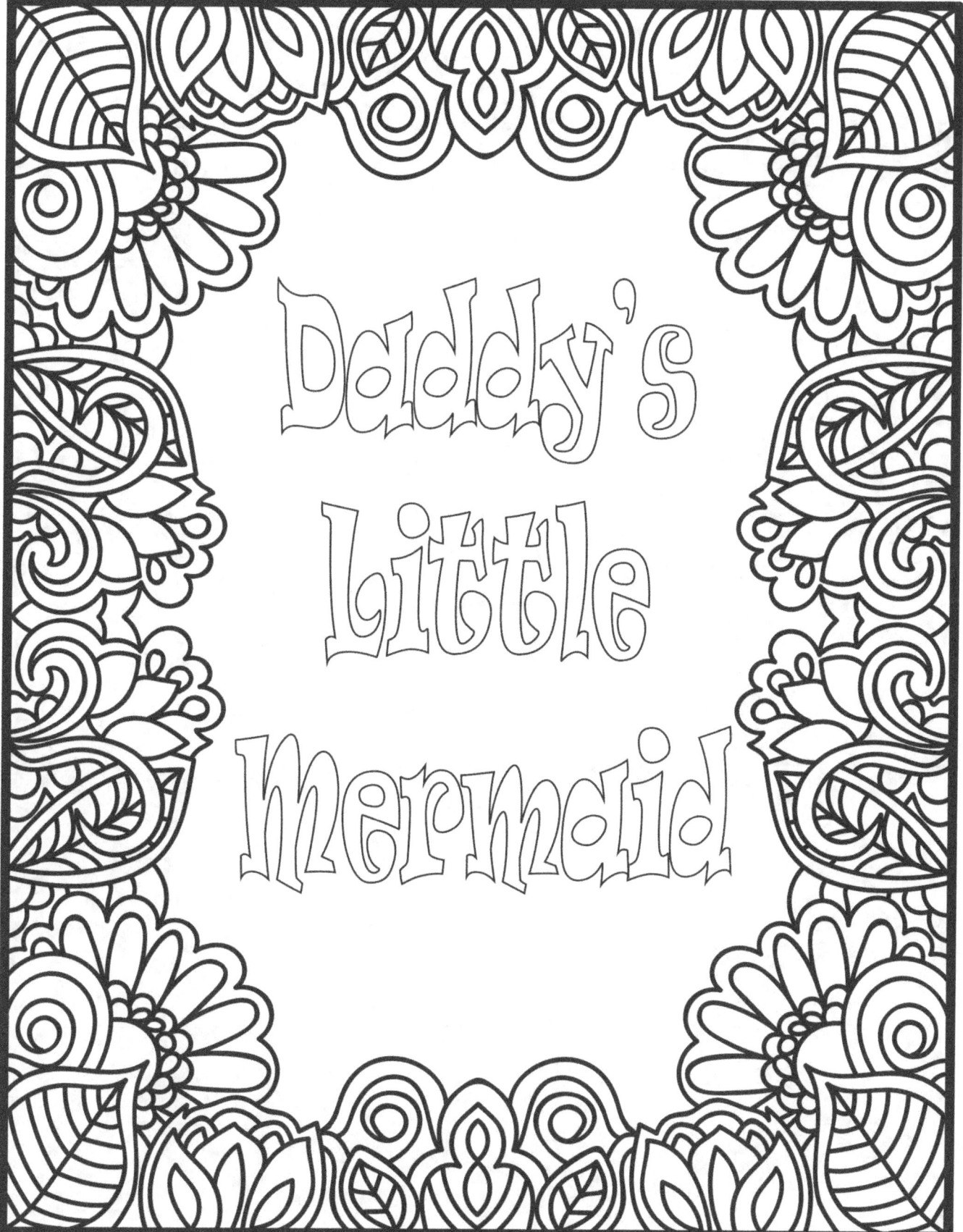

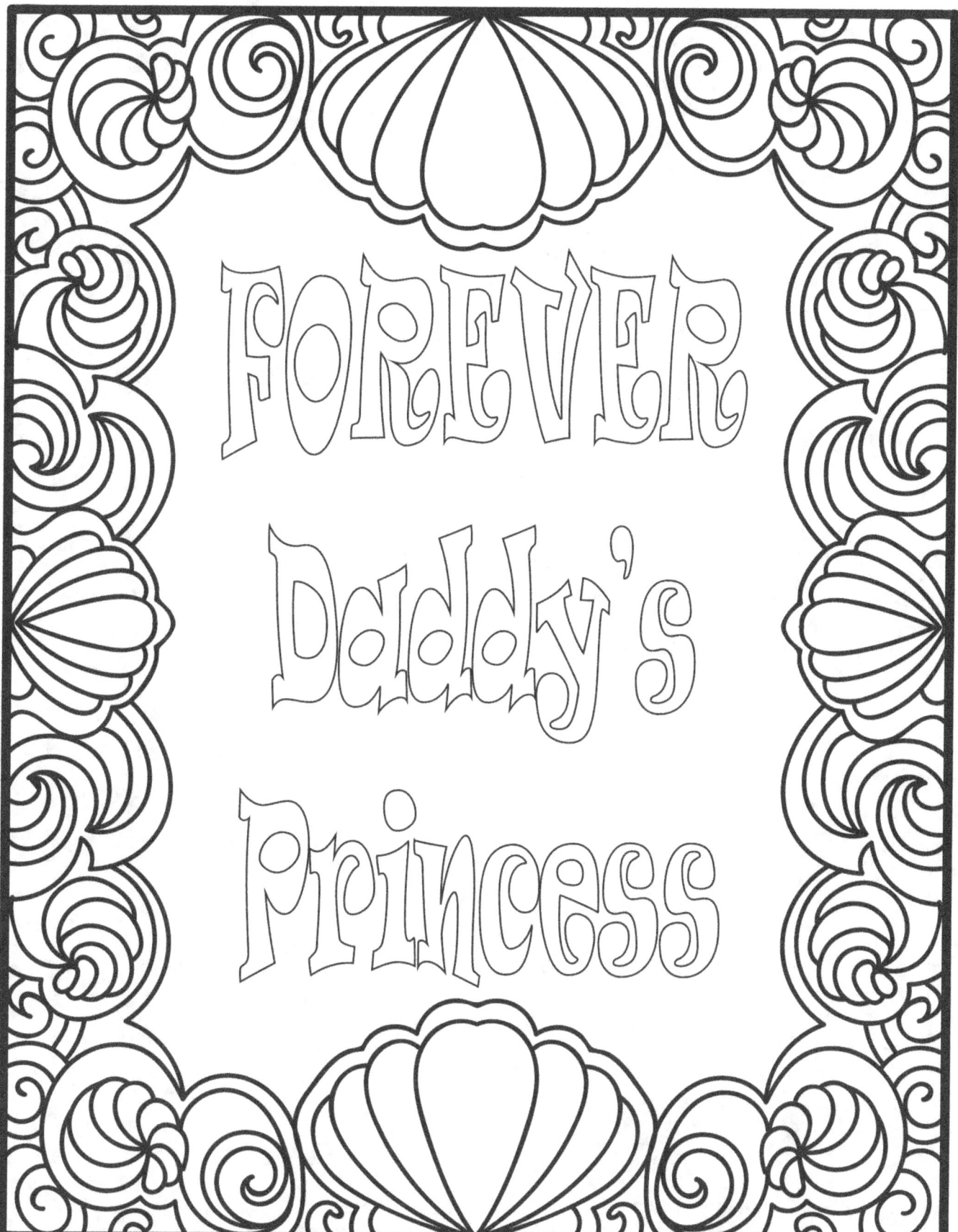

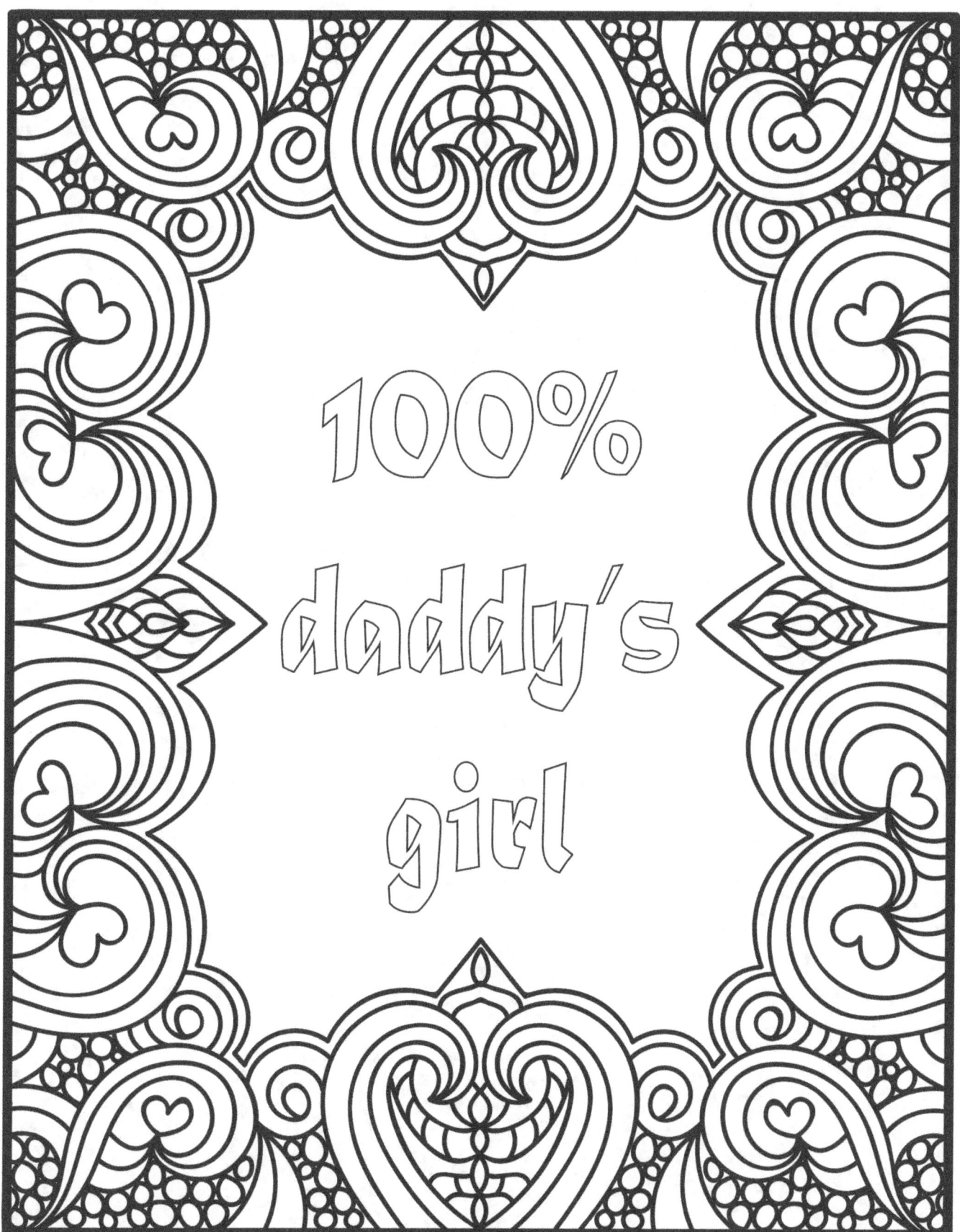

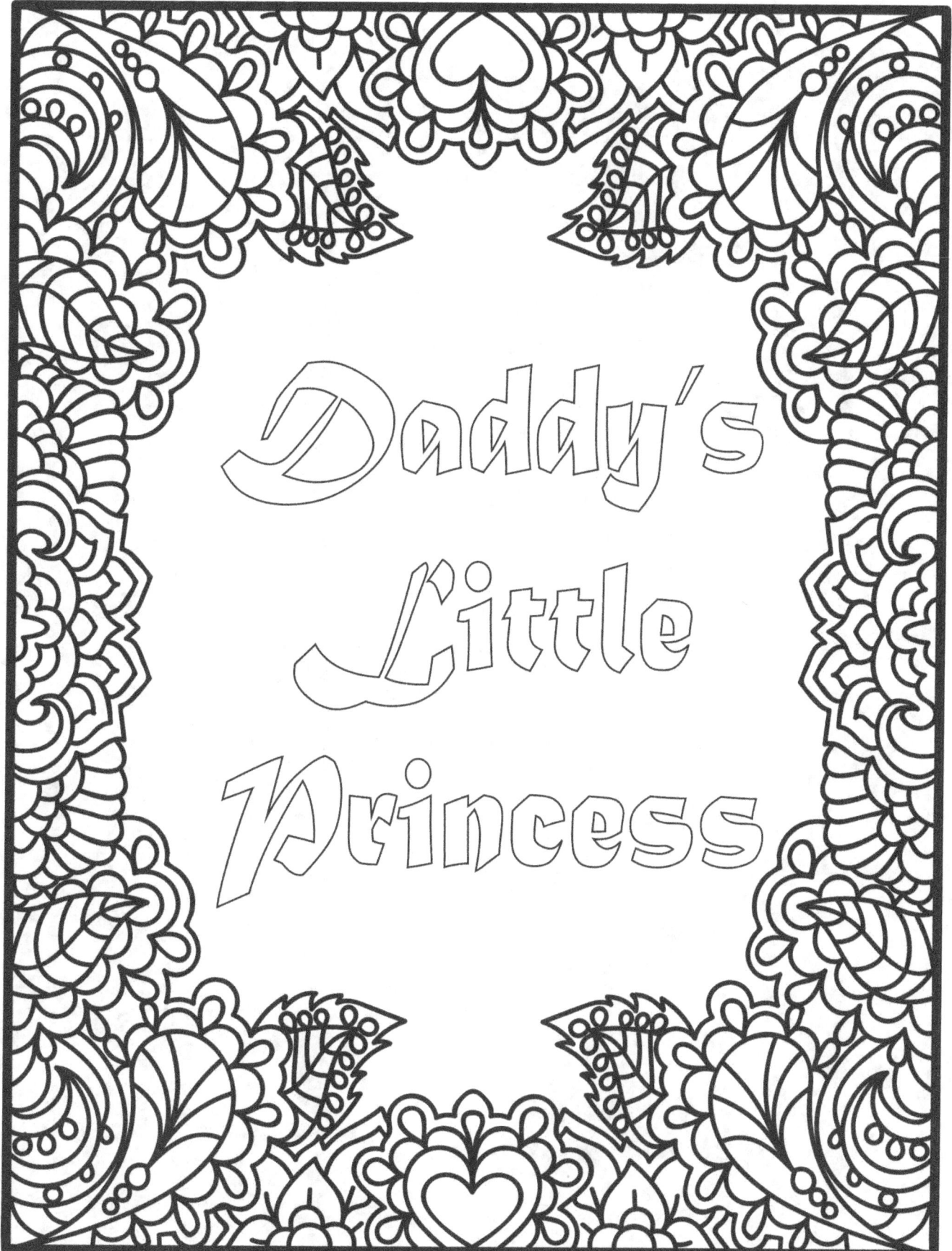

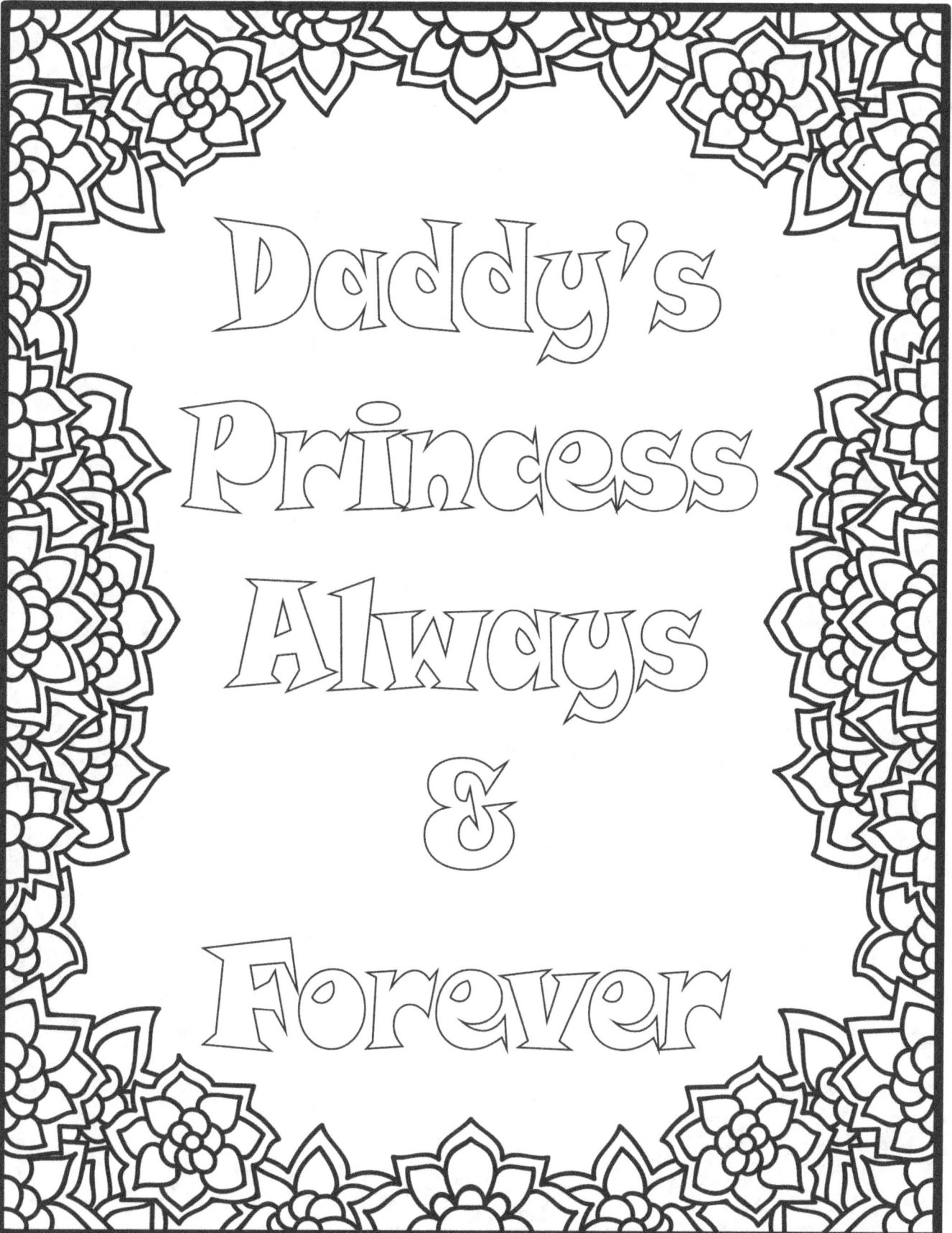

COLOR TEST PAGE

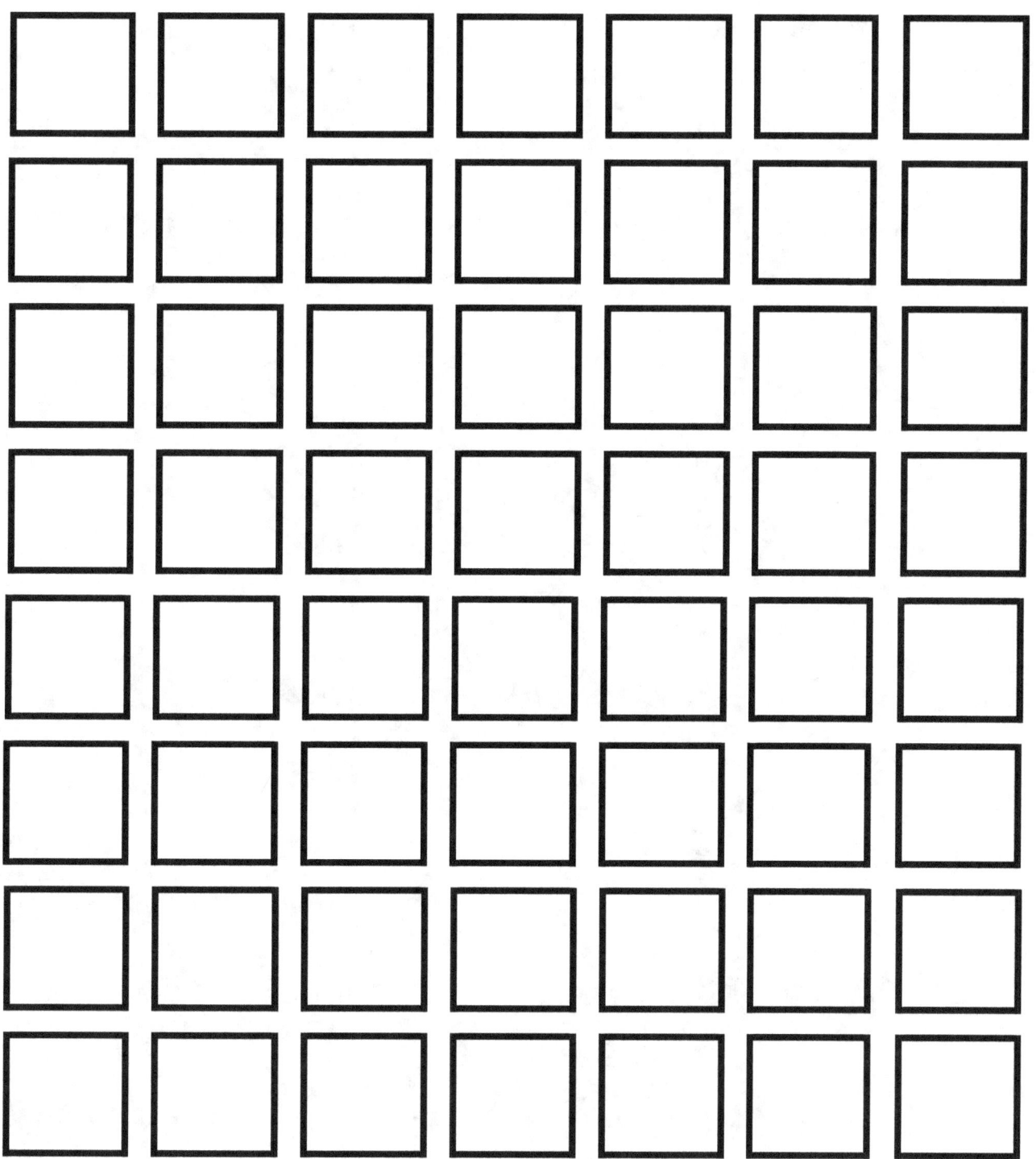

COLOR TEST PAGE

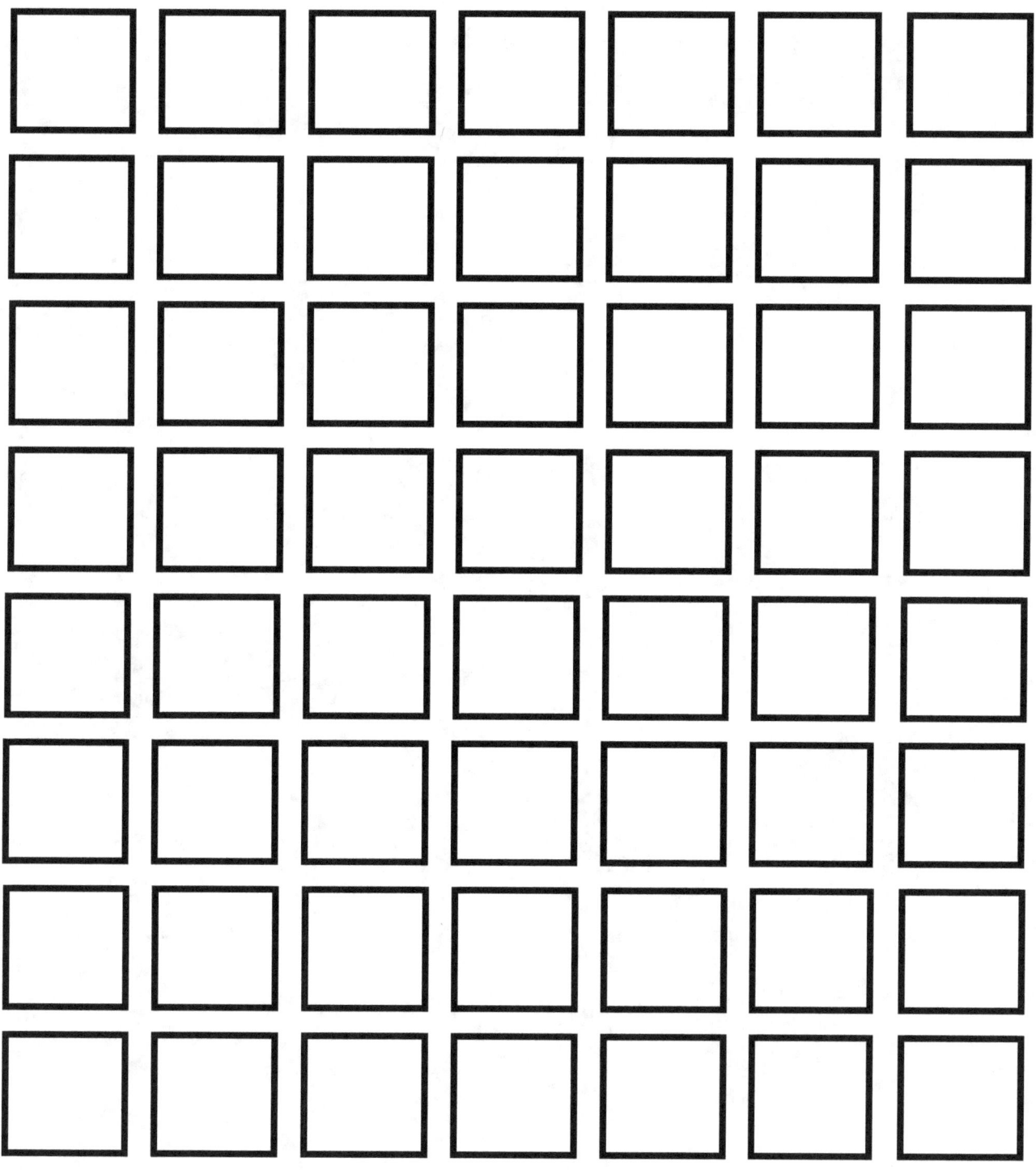

www.ingramcontent.com/pod-product-compliance
Lightning Source LLC
Chambersburg PA
CBHW081615220526
45468CB00010B/2889